S&D MEMORIES

Compiled by Alan Hammond

Millstream Books

First published 1993
Millstream Books
7 Orange Grove
Bath BA1 1LP

© Alan Hammond 1993

This book set by Ryburn Typesetting, Keele University
Printed by The Matthews Wright Press, Chard

ISBN 0-948975-36-9

Masbury Station: the 1963 big freeze. A view from the cab of 3F No 47276 looking up towards the summit (John Stamp)

The cover map is by Duncan Harper and is available as a print from the above address.

LIST OF CONTRIBUTORS

The contents of this book are arranged as a journey down the line and branch. This list serves as an index.

Broadstone signalbox 2/5/65 (Colin Caddy)

Chargeman fitter Howard Hiscox seated at his desk at Bath Green Park shed during the last years of the S&D
(John Stamp)

INTRODUCTION & ACKNOWLEDGEMENTS

I was a keen railway enthusiast when I was younger and my interest was rekindled after seeing the television film *Return to Evercreech Junction.* I became enthralled with this railway. On a family holiday in Somerset I visited Washford, home of the S&DR Trust, where coincidentally a staff reunion was taking place. I was fascinated by all that was going on around me and it was apparent that they had a real love of the job. I wanted to know more about the people who worked and loved this railway.

I decided to send a questionnaire to as many of those who worked on the S&D as I could asking them for their memories. Bearing in mind that I did not know the people nor want to pry into something that for many was a special part of their life, I took the plunge and, with the help of my wife Christine, sent out 30 questionnaires.

The response was quite extraordinary and I was astounded and thrilled enough to send out 200 more requests over the next 18 months. I was also welcomed into their homes with my tape recorder to record their memories.

A number of them suggested that I should try to compile a book. Some stories are unprintable and many have had to be left out but I have tried to emphasise the personal recollections of the line by the people who worked it. These are genuine memories of events that happened up to 70 years ago.

I would like to thank all those kind people who have given me stories and photographs and helped with information. Particular thanks are due to: Bruce Masters for initial encouragement; Len Barry, whose help on the photographic side has been so important; Laurie Poulton of the S&D Trust East Anglian group for his kind help with access through the group to the J F Rimmer collection; Mrs May Rimmer for the photographs of her late husband; Les Willsher and Will Locke, whose phone calls and letters have inspired me greatly. Also special thanks to Fred and Joan Fisher, Maurice and Norah Cook, Percy Hobbs, John Stamp, Bill May, Gordon Hatcher, John Sawyer and Eddie Skinner.

Sadly, some of those who answered the questionnaire have now passed away and I would like to thank the families of Dorothy Down, Frank Packer, Ron Bean, Fred Davis, Eddie Jackson and David Massey.

I must mention the Somerset & Dorset Railway Trust, for without them I would never have been introduced to the S&D. Many photographers have allowed me access to their collections – their skills have brought lasting memories of the S&D for us to enjoy. My thanks to my publishers Alan Summers, Tim Graham and Andy Moon for their help and professional advice, and a special thank you to Roy Pitman of the Trust who kindly put me in touch with all the former staff who appear in this book.

Last but not least, my wife Christine has somehow deciphered my handwriting and transferred it onto word processor – she has been a pillar of strength to me and a great help.

Finally, this publication is dedicated to all the men and women, past and present, who worked on the Somerset & Dorset Joint Railway. An old signalman said to me "The S&D was a family". I have been very fortunate to have met part of that family – I hope you will enjoy meeting them too.

Alan Hammond   July 1993

BATH

Archie Gunning

My family has been involved with the railway since 1880, when my father Emmanuel Gunning joined the Midland Railway. He got married in the late 1880s and moved to a railway house in Hopmead Buildings, Bath. He lived there with his family until 1918 when he moved into Dorset Street. He always worked in the permanent way department and eventually rose to be a ganger in the Weston-Bitton length, finally ending his career on the S&D as a member of the Bath gang. He retired in the late 1930s and passed away in 1952 at the grand old age of 84.

My elder brother Bill joined the S&D soon after the First World War, and was a colleague of that well known driver Donald Beale. He was persuaded by an uncle, who was also a driver, to join the railway in the glamour job, on the footplate. Bill was at Bath Green Park all his S&D railway career including the war period and took retirement upon the closure of the S&D in 1966 where he had risen to senior driver. He died in the early 1970s.

My other brother Tom followed Bill into the railway at Bath Green Park in 1921. Unfortunately he was laid off several times in the 1920s. He spent some time on loan to Highbridge shed, but eventually took his place as a fireman at Bath Green Park in the early 1930s.

Promotion to driver came before the war and he worked through various links as time progressed. The closure of the S&D at Bath Green Park in 1966 meant Tom was transferred to Bristol where he drove prestige trains like the "Blue Pullman". He retired at the age of 63, Tom and myself still regularly have a natter about the old times on the S&D. The Gunning family tradition on the S&D continued when Bill's son Reg joined the S&D, just before World War Two. I remember him firing to me when he was just a 16 year old lad. He climbed the ladder from a passed cleaner and ended up as a top link driver at Bristol, where he retired in 1987.

My first introduction to the S&D was as a boy on illicit footplate rides with my brother Bill, which I thoroughly enjoyed. When I joined the S&D on the 10th March 1929 I was just 15 years of age. When I arrived for work I was put with the steamraiser, the job consisted of cleaning the firebox bars, tube plates and also bringing down coal from the engine's tender. I continued with this for a short time then I moved on to be a call boy, which meant calling up all the drivers and firemen at night. The hours were from 12pm till 7am, not a very nice job for a young man, but it had to be done. I progressed to an engine cleaner with three other lads.

I remember on one occasion working with the coalman. His mate never turned up for work, so I was put in his job at the coal stage; what a job, filling in coal tubs and engine tenders, that was really hard work.

I continued with my cleaning duties, when I had a message from the shedmaster that they had a job for me at Bristol working with the blacksmith. I stayed there for about 18 months, and then returned to Bath and started on the promotion ladder.

From passed cleaner I then became a fireman. A lot of work had to go into becoming a fireman. To achieve this I was doing more and more firing jobs, working rest days to get as much experience as possible. The war had just started and I was put into the passenger link, I worked from Bath to Templecombe for a few months, and was then put into the S&D goods link; promotion was nearly there. I was called into the office to see the inspector, he explained what was ahead in the next few weeks. He gave me a tough time. I also went to mutual improvement classes on Sunday mornings, the old drivers used to take them, they were a great help.

Examination day came along, part of the test was to name all of the parts from the buffer to the back of the engine, and to explain where the oiling points were. I also had to drive a goods train from Bath to Evercreech Junction, and return to Bath with a passenger train. I achieved 70 marks out of 100 and became a passed fireman in 1941, later to qualify as a driver. Finally I entered the top link in 1964.

Looking back at all the different jobs that I had in my early days on the S&D it certainly helped me understand the railway.

Driver Archie Gunning and fireman Albert Parsons on the footplate of BR class 4 2-6-4T No 80041 at Bath Green Park after working the 2pm from Templecombe, Feb 1966 (John Stamp)

Ron Gray

My career on the S&D started on the 14th July 1934 at Bath Green Park, at 6am on a Saturday. My wages were 16 shillings a week, when you reached the age of 16 it went up to a £1. I was employed as a bar boy and also helped to get the coal for the steamraiser who was your mate. When the engines were cold you had to climb into the fireboxes to clean the tube plates, crown stays, brick arches and fire bars, if any fire bars wanted changing, you had to carry this out. Each firebox was examined by a boilersmith, ours being William Salvage.

After three years I was promoted to an engine cleaner, I was then 17 years of age; in those days you could not be a fireman until you were 18.

In March 1938 I started firing and I was then classified as a passed cleaner, which meant I could be used as a fireman. To reach the grade of fireman you had to do 313 firing turns which I achieved in early 1940. Before you were allowed to go onto the main line you had to do relief work or go into the shunting and banking link to get experience of how to use a shovel. I fired to a lot of the old drivers: Bill Hooper, Bill Amos, Fred Lessey, Danny Alexandra, Charlie Crocker and Harold Barber; legends in their own right.

In 1943 I was passed out for driving, in those days you had to be 23 before you could go out driving. My first driving job was on a Sunday – it was a beautiful summer's evening, the 5pm from Bath and, being wartime, it was a hush hush job.

It turned out to be an American troop train, we had to work it to Templecombe then it was going on to a further destination unknown to us. It was a double header, and in them days the oldest experienced driver would be on the leading engine because of the braking. His name was Fred Brooks. We had 12 bogies on. We pulled away from Bath Green Park with 21 inches of vacuum. When we got to Bath Junction the brakes went on. We went back down to 15 inches of vacuum.

Fred came back to me and informed us that we had got vacuum trouble, it was a journey never to be forgotten. We stopped three times between Bath and Midford. By then we had all had enough. The train came to a halt at Midford outer home signal again. Driver Fred Brooks the guard and myself went and saw the American commanding officer. Walking through the train we could see what the problem was, the troops were tying their kit bags to the communication cord. Once we had sorted this out with their senior officer and explained why they couldn't do it we then made haste to Templecombe arriving there 1½ hours late.

A funny incident that sticks in my mind, when I was firing to a driver called Percy Bromley, began at Bournemouth on a lodging turn. We left Bournemouth for Bath and Percy took his shoes off. When we arrived at Bath he couldn't get his shoes back on: the shoes had shrunk on the footplate! He was too embarrassed to go into the lobby and book off. We had a foreman there called Tom Rudd and when I went in there he said to me "Where's your driver then, sonny?" I said "he's coming". I went and saw a railwayman who was an ambulance man he let me into the first aid hut to borrow a wheelchair. I had to push him home to Fairview in Twerton. To my knowledge the foreman never found out. We laughed about this for ages.

Mike Ryall

As a passed fireman you had what we called links at Bath Green Park, ranging from shunting and banking to the top passenger link. I was in the spare link where we would cover rest day work, which would be goods one day and passenger the next. The duties would vary, sometimes you would come on duty with the engine already prepared to go onto the main line, other times you would come on and prepare your own engine. There was also shed duties, where you would have to prepare and dispose of a number of engines. To prepare a engine would take about an hour.

As a fireman my duties would start when I climbed onto the footplate; you would first check how much steam you had, then check your boiler for water. You would then get a fire iron down from the tender and push out the fire and put the blower on to raise steam. Whilst this was going on you would check your tools, which consisted of a shovel, bucket and fire irons made up of a rake, chisel bar and a shovel all long enough to reach the end of the firebox. On a freight train they were placed on the tender on special racks, whilst on a passenger train like the Black 5s there was a special compartment for them, in either case it wanted some manoeuvring to get them out of the racks and into the fire.

First you had to make sure that there were no road bridges or tunnels approaching, as well as looking out for any trains coming in the opposite direction. It was even harder putting them back because of them being red hot. Also you would have three spanners. One of them would be a large ⅞: this was to tighten up the smokebox door. You should also have a canister of 12 detonators and two red flags. You would then climb out of the cab with the ⅞ spanner along the outer footplate cleaning the window first, then check the sand boxes on that side, and then go around to the front and tighten up the smokebox if required. Then you would do the same on the other side of the engine. You would look at the fire, put some coal on and by then your driver should have finished his checking and oiling. He would then move the engine forward under the water column whilst the tender is being filled up with water. You would fill the firebox up with coal, swill down the coal dust and wash down the cab with what we call the slacking pipe, which was situated on the fireman's side with a tap at one end and a handle on the other, surrounded by a little coil. On the tender were two compartments – one for you and your driver to put your grub boxes in and the other for housing oil and paraffin cans for filling up the head and tail lights.

In the men's messroom at Bath Green Park there was a large open fireplace where some of the cleaners, especially those on nights would stack the coal half way up the chimney, so that when the coal did burn through the walls of the outside were glowing red hot.

At Bath Green Park the summers were the most busiest times, especially on Saturdays, we used to get locomotive staff from Radstock to help out mainly on shed duties. It was on one of these occasions that a serious accident occurred in 1959. It involved a Radstock driver and a West Country class loco. The driver was not too conversant with this type of loco. He moved the engine from under the coal stage (which was also called No 2 road), forward up a slight incline, stopped, pulled the hand points to go onto the next road which was No 3 and had an ash pit for cleaning out fires. There was a wagon over the pit and a class 7F not in steam behind it up against the buffers. Immediately behind them was the foreman cleaner's office which was like a sentry box, next to that was the men's messroom. The poor old Radstock driver proceeded down the incline but could not stop his engine. It gathered speed and hit the wagon that was over the pit shunting the dead engine back into the buffers snapping them in half. It went straight into the foreman's office smashing it to bits, then into the wall of the messroom where it came to a standstill. Fortunately nobody was hurt even though there was a driver sat by this wall in the messroom, whom I understand moved like greased lightning down to the far end of the messroom up onto the sink and out through the window as the doorway was down the other end of the room where the wall had buckled.

Bernard Ware

It was a happy time at Bath Junction signalbox; Bill Wilds worked there and was a very jovial character. He came from Stalbridge. Bert Henman was another mate; he came from the Birmingham area and he went on to become the local signalman inspector. I often wondered if he ever checked signalmen as to whether they got up to the tricks that he did. When he was a signalman he was known to cut men's hair: one day he was giving a permanent way man a trim, when he noticed the signalman inspector approaching. There was a mad dash, the permanent way man running up the line his hair cut only on one side, and Bert hurriedly clearing his hair-cutting tackle away. Bert also mended watches and clocks: one night at 10pm when I relieved Bill Wilds in the box, I said to Bill "What's that ticking?" Bill turned round and said "It's only one of Bert's clocks on test in his locker". Being the joker he was he had picked a time when it was quiet that night and I was taking it easy with one eye shut when this alarm on this clock in the locker went off. I jumped up a little scared at first and then realized what was happening. That's the kind of chap he was.

Charlie Davies talking to Bert Veasey. Bert Illott (back to camera) with Midland taillamp. Bernard Ware looks on – note the Western handlamp on platform (Bernard Ware collection)

Richard Kelson

Although I was only on the S&D for a few years it has held everlasting memories for me. I was 16 when I turned up at Bath Green Park. I was recommended for the job by Ralph Holden junior, whom I became acquainted with whilst doing farm work. His father Ralph senior and brother Doug also worked at the Bath motor power depot. I started as a cleaner. Other workmates who started at around that time were Roger Dyte, Tony Pitt, Cyril Gould, Tony Cox and quite a few others; they were a great bunch of lads.

We were detailed in gangs to clean the engines by Fred Trimm, the shed foreman: at that time you would work three shifts – 8am to 4pm, 4pm to 12pm and 12pm to 8am. We had a different foreman on nights, one being Cyril Bruton. We would carry out the cleaning we were allocated and then spend the rest of the shift trying to keep out of the way of the shed foreman.

Most crews were only too glad to have somebody to clean out the smokebox or rake out an ash pan for you. If they were short of a coalman on the stage, or were very busy, volunteers would be called for to assist loading wagons and coaling engines; this was very hard and dirty work. We would also help in emptying the ash pits and loading ash into the wagons.

Another memory I have was working a freight train with an old driver called Bunny (I believe his name was Fred Hemmings). This was an early morning turn and we were stuck on shed for a long time, so we had a fry up on the shovel which included kippers; I can still smell and taste them now, lovely grub! The messroom at Bath had a big fireplace and coal being in plentiful supply meant we always had a big fire, sometimes so big it would be too hot to sit anywhere near it. One or two of the younger element would build it up on purpose. We had wooden benches and tables and screwed to one of them was a shove ha-penny board. This was made of slate and used to get a lot of use. I think most of the staff became very good at sitting down and playing with either hand.

Also at Bath one of the clerks Arthur Polden was very proficient at removing coal dust or ash from eyes. He would stand you up against a wall, turn the eyelid right back and remove the dust. I think he used to do this with a piece of bent wire.

I remember going to the Youth Club which was organized by Burt Hulonce. The club was situated on the Lower Bristol Road, Bath which was by the Green Park Tavern, we used to go there to play records and skittles. I also remember driver Frank Redfern the union official for ASLEFF who collected the union dues on pay day, a nice bloke was Frank. I left the S&D in 1960 to do my National Service, and never returned to the railway.

MIDFORD

John Sawyer

A task for the fireman was preparing the automatic Whitaker tablet catcher, for the taking and collecting of the small pouch. This was fairly easy at Bath Junction compared to Midford. Collecting the large pouch at Midford en route to Bath from the signalman was a different story. Travelling at speed, leaning out of the side of the cab, hanging on to the hand rail with one hand, and about to lunge your other hand through the large ring attached to the pouch was to say the least a bit frightening at times, especially if you had a train of coal on behind you. Also of course going through your mind is, if I miss this flaming pouch or drop it you'd be in trouble, your driver would certainly not be too pleased with you. It would mean stopping the train and reversing it back up around the curve to Midford, up distant signal and then trying again, and of course you had the knock-on effect of trains running late for the rest of the day. Quite a lot of responsibility for a lad of 17 years of age.

Bill Harford

I joined the S&D at Branksome on 12th May 1952 as a cleaner. We did not carry out much cleaning but was expected to assist the firemen when they came on shed. We also helped the steamraisers with cleaning out the running pits and keeping the shed in a clean and tidy condition. After a couple of weeks I was made a passed cleaner which meant I could fire to Templecombe and back.

I remember the first time I went to Bath we took a West Country class light engine back to Bath for repairs, I was firing to driver Bill Bailey. When we approached the Mendips it was thick fog and at night you couldn't see anything.

It was quite a ghostly feeling especially going light engine with just the flames from the fire for company. Fortunately Bill had worked on this line for many years and knew every inch of it, which was handy that night when arriving at Midford home signal which was on. After a couple of minutes Bill sent me forward to the signalbox to sign the book for Rule 55. He suggested that I walk along the cess (which is on the side of the track) to the box which he told me was on the station. It was my first time over Midford. I gingerly got out of the cab and made my way over the viaduct towards the signalbox. The fog was as thick as pea soup. After a few yards I could see nothing and was completely disorientated, I kept moving hoping that I was going in the right direction, when suddenly I came to the side of the viaduct and almost fell over the top. After a couple of deep breaths and gaining my composure I started walking again and finally saw the light of Midford signalbox. It was the best sight I had ever seen. I went up into the box, signed the book and made my way back carefully to the West Country engine making sure I could see the track at all times.

The next time I went to Bath in daylight and saw how high the viaduct was I felt quite shocked. At 17 years of age walking across Midford viaduct in pitch darkness and thick fog is something I never ever wanted to repeat.

Arthur King

The incident that stands out in my mind most happened in 1942. I was the fireman on the 2.40am mail to Bournemouth from Bath. On this turn you came back the same evening working a freight train from Bournemouth West yard which normally was not a very heavy load, but on this particular night the London line had been bombed, the train had to be diverted via the S&D to Bath and the Midlands. This was a very heavy train and we had a Black 5 No 5440, my driver was Les Bailey, he was on loan to Bath from the Midlands, I believe he was from the Leicester area. We left Bournemouth at 9.30pm that night and made our way to Bath, I had to work very hard and we burnt a lot of coal, as you will see later in this story. All went well until we reached Midford. As we approached I did the usual thing which was to get the long rake or pricker out of the tender and level the fire over the firebox, so it would not leave too much fire running into Bath (for the fire to be cleaned on shed) this left an incandescent fire which was very hot. My driver opened up and got the train running at a fair speed through the dip at Midford whilst I got the single line tablet out of the catcher on the tender. We now climbed up the 1 in 50 gradient to Combe Down tunnel. This tunnel is well over a mile long, single lined and no ventilators. The chimney misses the roof by about three inches. When we were about three quarters through the tunnel 5440 decided to slip, which the driver could not stop. We finally came to a halt.

As I had full pressure of steam and the fire being so hot, the safety valves blew off steam. This hit the low roof and came straight down into the cab and, with the sulphur fumes from the chimney, it became unbearable. Les decided that as we could not go forward, because the engine could not get away, we would run back out, but this we could not do as the guard being an old goods guard had put his brake in the van hard on, thinking we had a Class 7F freight engine. He would take it off as soon as he felt a tug of the train starting away and all would be well, but as it was we could go neither backwards or forwards. We could not stand being on the footplate any longer so we both got down on the engine steps where it was cooler although still very unpleasant. After a while the guard

Midford Station May 1965: less than a year to go to closure – how clean and tidy everything is (Colin Caddy)

realized there was something wrong and took his brake off, we ran back outside where I got on the phone to the signalman who gave us permission to run back and have another go. This we did and pushed the train up the bank the other side as far as we could, to get a run at the tunnel again. I swept the tender clean of coal as we had none left, this time we went through with no problems and ran into Bath's goods reception line, cut off and went over to the turntable to turn, as all engines have to at Bath before going to the shed. A shunter came over to see us and asked who the guard was. We told him it's Billy Howell, he said he was not in his van. When the shunting engine came up behind to shunt the engine into the yard, it would not move as the brake was hard on.

The guard had for some reason put his brake on and got out of the van at Midford when we had pushed it back, so although we could not pull the train through the first time, we did the second time with the brake hard on and no guard! By the way, we were both off work for a while after as the heat had burnt our lungs. I am glad to say I have not had any trouble with them since.

Cliff Smith

I was a passed fireman on a goods train waiting at Midford to go onto the single line to Bath. I picked my wife a bunch of cowslips at Evercreech. At Midford I saw some violets on the embankment so I got off the engine to pick some to go with the cowslips. I picked about a dozen when something moved by my hand. It was an adder and it was about six inches from my hand. I was back on that engine faster than an olympic runner!

George Skinner

One Saturday morning whilst working a train to Bath, the engine had no exchanging gear as it was from the North. All went well and we exchanged by hand the pouch with a big steel ring, until we approached Midford. Of course by this time we had a pilot engine in front and the young driver had forgotten we had no catcher. I reminded the driver that we were approaching the signalbox at speed, he replied "Well take it by hand". I was too long in the tooth to obey such an order and I told him so, he stood and shouted "Well stand aside, I'll do it" he held onto the footplate handle and put out his arm. I can still hear the whack now. When we got to Bath his arm was black and blue.

WELLOW

Mike Baker

There was a turn when we would work the last train down from Bath to Templecombe, in the 1960s there was Sputniks satellites to be seen in the sky at night. After leaving Midford I spotted one and pointed it out to the driver, we watched the satellite and as we proceeded around the curves we would be going from one side of the footplate to the other, sometimes watching it through the open cab roof shutter. On this trip we suddenly both realized we had become completely disorientated and didn't know where we were. The driver was sure we had run through Wellow without stopping. Fortunately a few moments later Wellow station loomed out of the darkness, so all was well.

Frank Staddon

My first memory of Wellow was when I was a young child. I used to go there bank holidays with my father. He used to say to me "you better save up those pennies", which I did. It used to cost 10 pennies return from Binegar to Wellow in them days. I joined the S&D in May 1935 and remember working at Wellow, I was a district relief porter and worked there in the war years. It was a lovely station

Wellow 1960s: a view from the down platform looking towards the signalbox and foot crossing (J F Rimmer)

situated in picturesque countryside. It had various station buildings and a fair sized signalbox with a footpath crossing. I used to arrive at Wellow about 7am and around about 8.30 Harry Wiltshire the signalman would shout out "tea up

Wellow signalbox with wicket gate in the foreground – an idyllic setting on a summer's day (J F Rimmer)

Frank". Harry and I would have a natter and enjoy our tea in the box. The day was spent making sure the station was clean and tidy, looking after the home and distant signals. It was handy in the summer months, when you went to attend the down distant you could always pick yourselves a pocket full of fresh mushrooms in the field nearby.

You always had to be in attendance because it was necessary to shunt goods trains. We were kept busy by a fellow working up in Wellow village: he used to send out a lot of wheel barrows. There was a small ground frame that you had to work to control the goods wagons.

I recall an occasion when a couple of miners got off the Radstock train with a couple of sacks.

I guessed what they were up to; they were going to do a bit of poaching on a nearby estate at Wellow. After a couple of hours they returned. I walked over to them and asked what they had in these now bulging bags. They answered "just our little dogs". Their dogs were whippets. "How about a rabbit then", I said, "I'll pay for it". One of them turned around and said "you're not having any rabbits". "Fine", I said "in that case I'll make you pay for a dog ticket" which was three pennies back to Radstock, which I did. I wasn't very popular after this.

At that time the signalman took in outward bound telegrams. It was the porter's job to deliver them. On one occasion Harry gave me this telegram for a house about two miles away. I managed to find this house after walking across a field, but could not find the gate, so I decided to vault over a wall and landed in two feet of pigs manure... then I found out that it was the wrong house!

Bernard Ware

I returned to the S&D about March 1946 as a summer relief signalman class 2 based at Bath Green Park. I had been working the previous five years as a signalman in the Birmingham region. I should add that our area went from Bailey Gate to the other side of Birmingham and branches of the Midland section.

For a period of time I was a signalman at Wellow box on holiday relief during the summer months. It had the usual signals in both directions; namely distant home starter and advance starter. There was no track circuits and no locks on the block instruments, as was the case on the LMS. I believe to shunt a short freight train into the up sidings the guard would pull a lever which gave an indication in the signalbox. The signalman would then pull a lever which enabled the guard to work the points for the train to shunt into the up sidings. One thing that stands out in my memory at that time was dealing with Post Office telegrams, people would come to the signalbox at Wellow to send a telegram. We would then send it on to Bath Post Office. Sometimes a telegram would be received from Bath control for someone in Wellow village. You would put it into an envelope and call the porter to the signalbox. He would then deliver it.

SHOSCOMBE & SINGLE HILL HALT

Frank Staddon
Shoscombe and Single Hill halt was built for the miners and their families in

1929. There were many collieries around this area. Braysdown and Writhlington were two of them that I recall. The halt over a period of many years was looked after by the Chivers family, more recently by two sisters. The family had a real S&D history, members of the family worked as shunters, signalmen, and also on the permanent way.

Shoscombe & Single Hill Halt: a view from the down platform looking towards Wellow. Note the waiting shelter in left background. The halt was a Southern Railway standard concrete construction (J F Rimmer)

I was a district relief porter located at Bath Green Park and my travels took me to Shoscombe halt. On one occasion that I recall I was sent there for one week to take over from Mrs Chivers who was going on her annual holiday. The porter's job was to see in all the trains, to unload any goods and more importantly to ensure the signal lamps were on and working. The halt came under the control of the Radstock stationmaster Mr Lewis who was well known as a loyal company man. On the Monday morning at Shoscombe halt I was met by Mr Lewis, I had travelled down on the first available train which was the 7am. He informed me that I could not book to lodge there for the week, but had to travel daily. As he was the stationmaster I carried out his instructions to the letter. Well early on the Tuesday morning 25 passengers (a Sunday school outing) travelled on the first down passenger, with no tickets (there was nobody there to give them their tickets). This was reported by the ticket inspector George Quinn. Once Mr Lewis heard about this he came straight down on the next train and informed me that I could now book to lodge, which entitled me to three shillings a day lodge expenses. I was quite pleased about this, bearing in mind your duties did not finish at the halt until 6.30pm.

RADSTOCK

John Sawyer

I recall an incident in the 1960's that I was involved in at Writhlington colliery. I was on the 7am relief at Bath Green Park, and the fireman had failed to report for duty at Radstock shed so I was despatched on the next passenger train to Radstock to undertake his duties. On arrival at Radstock shed the driver had prepared the engine himself and was eagerly awaiting my arrival so that we could get underway with the day's work. I got on the footplate and we proceeded to Writhlington colliery. That was about 8am. My first job was to pull coal wagons out of the colliery and into the sidings. We pulled about 10 wagons and dropped them into the sidings but on returning to get some more we became derailed. Well my first thought was why did I bother coming into work, and only being about 17 years of age I had visions of a shift lasting longer than eight hours and missing my night out.

But the S&D being what it was, it wasn't long before the driver, guard, shunter and myself plus the help of about a dozen wooden sleepers had it back on the track in about two hours. We continued our work and I got home about 4pm, to my knowledge nobody else except us four and the Radstock signalman knew anything at all about what went on that day.

Frank Sealy

Another memory though somewhat hazy is from 1926 when the general strike was called. Mr Whitaker, my father and another chap took a perishable down over the S&D and it caused a bit of a furore in the Somerset coalfields at Radstock. It also caused a lot of aggravation in the family as it was considered that they were strike breaking and we were supposed to be emerging socialists in 1926.

Bert Short

I remember being on the footplate of one of the old oil burning Black 5's which had been converted from coal. The order was to sand the tubes which we could from the cab with a sand box and wheel on an up gradient when the engine was really working its limit. On passing Radstock towards Midsomer Norton we performed our duty, the wheel was shut down after a couple of minutes. It was amusing to us, I don't know about the people of Radstock; when I looked back a cloud hung over Radstock blocking out most of the houses, and over our heads was a lovely blue sky. The cloud was just like a big black umbrella, I thought there would be complaints from the ladies of Radstock about their washing but I never heard anything.

Frank Staddon

I spent 43 years on the railway, mostly on the S&D, and my final position was as a conductor guard. Luckily I finished my railway career without a serious accident. But one close shave was when working a coal train with 22 wagons on from Midsomer Norton to Bath. We had the distant signal at Radstock and my driver Reg Beasley opened up the regulator and set sail. On the platform at Radstock I saw a permanent way man frantically waving a red flag. I grabbed up the brake stick, slammed on the brake and then an almighty thump landed me at the far end of the brake van. I couldn't see anything for dust. My driver Reg came running back and was relieved to see me shaken but not injured. What had happened was that the permanent way men had not notified the signalmen at Radstock that they had taken a rail out. All praise to Reg and his driving that he had stopped the train with just yards to spare.

Fred Fisher

I remember when I was on a West Country class Pacific No 34043 "Combe Martin" with a class 2 on the front. I was firing to my regular mate Charlie Gould, we were running into Radstock when our engine caught alight. She was in a bad way. We came to a standstill at Radstock and I protected the opposite running road. I uncoupled the engine and we put it into Writhlington coal sidings. We then worked the train onto Bath with the class 2. We were very lucky. If the fire had started while we were in Combe Down tunnel it would have turned into an extremely dangerous situation for the passengers and ourselves. Fortunately everything turned out alright in the end.

We used to come in contact with animals on the line. I recall I was on a passenger train with a class 2 engine when we knocked down a cow. What a mess. Fortunately for the animal it died instantly. We also used to run down a few pheasants. If we were on a freight train we would stop pick them up and take them home for our dinner.

Les Willsher

I joined the S&D on Easter Monday 1940 as a porter at Radstock. Mr Lewis was the stationmaster at that time. My duties were general platform work and I earned about £2 a week.

After nine months I moved on to Bath as a temporary guard where I had to learn the road to Templecombe, Evercreech, Bournemouth West and the branch to Burnham-on-Sea. I finally passed out as a guard and continued working at Bath.

Radstock level crossing Jan 1955 taken from the north signalbox. Note the Bedford CA pickup with builders' tilt in the back and also the Clandown branch off to the right on the up line (John Stamp)

Being in the war years we had to know what each individual siding could hold along the line in case a train had to be shunted and parted or when allowing express trains through during air raid warnings.

I well remember in April 1942 Bath was being bombed and 3 or 4 miles out of Bath people were sleeping out on banks and under hedges to escape the bombardment. I lived at Radstock and had to cycle 10 miles into Bath for the early turn where you had to arrive for work at 3am. I eventually made it into work and carried on with my duties as best as I could. In the same year I remember bringing in a train full of petrol into Bath when the sirens went off, fortunately nothing hit us and we continued into Bath.

Another memory that sticks in my mind was when we took a train to Evercreech. High up on the Mendips we could see Exeter was being bombed. The whole sky was lit up. I never forgot that sight.

Wartime working was dangerous, but as railwaymen we just got on with the job and battled through to make sure that ambulance trains, goods traffic and passenger services all reached their destinations. I always felt that the S&D did its bit in helping win the war.

I continued with my guard duties until 1946 when on 13th July working the Bath–Bournemouth West train I had a serious accident. We stopped at Blandford Forum to take water, the train was packed. I got off to make sure that no doors were left open. Then suddenly without me giving the hand signal to depart, the train started to move. I attempted to get back on the moving train, unfortunately I fell under one of the carriages. This resulted in me losing a leg. I was off work for over 2 years. I received £200 compensation and a disability pension of 7s6d per week. I was determined to get back to work so I learnt the rules and regulations to take up the position of a signalman at Masbury. For six weeks I was trained by a relief signalman Jack Bryant who helped me through. I stayed there for five years and then moved on to Radstock North in the 1950s when my cousin retired from the signalbox. It was a three shift box, with crossing gates open to road traffic, which caused a problem in the bad winter of 1963 when drifting snow made it extremely difficult to operate the gates.

I enjoyed my work at Radstock but in 1965 it was all coming to an end. We tried to save the line. I was the chief spokesman at Radstock and attended many meetings to try and save the S&D but to no avail. On Sunday March 6th 1966 I pulled the last lever at Radstock and said goodbye to the S&D which had been my life for 26 years.

Radstock Station 1960s: ten past one if the market clock is correct. A member of the station staff is concerned with the pram, possibly labelling it and not giving the one o'clock feed! The platform barrow is loaded with sacks (J F Rimmer)

MIDSOMER NORTON

Midsomer Norton: atmospheric view of the goods sidings and station. Note the Thornycroft parcels lorry in the yard – more Western influence! (J F Rimmer)

Ken Dando

Many years ago, before the war, I was cycling down the hill to Midsomer Norton. On reaching the station I saw a goods van with its buffers and a set of wheels standing on the boundary fence of the station. Two members of the staff were .looking at the scene and all I heard as I went past was "Aubrey has had an excess of zeal I see". Years later when working at Midsomer Norton I discovered who Aubrey was; he was an engine driver of an shunting engine and that particular morning had been shunting in the yard and had entered the shed road much too fast. New stop blocks were put in shortening the road. Originally three vans could be loaded beyond the shed, the new length meant that two vans stood clear, the third partly in the shed.

I worked as a clerk for many years at Midsomer Norton station and it was renowned for its station gardens. It had a green house and cold frame these were looked after by signalmen Fred Griffin, C Stevens and Joe Crouchen. The planting of the gardens was shared by the porters and signalmen, the grass being cut by anyone on the station who could find the time. In coronation year the gardens looked particularly beautiful with the theme being red, white and blue. All the staff did their best to make the station look good and it was noticed that the drivers of the "Pines Express" would slow down, so that the passengers could have a good look at the show of flowers. During the period when Mr L May was stationmaster, the station won many awards as the best kept station of its class.

In 1963 there was a very heavy snow fall. The lines were blocked beyond the Midsomer Norton signalbox on the down road. An engine made the journey to Radstock from Bath and it was decided that if the points could be cleared at Midsomer Norton the train service could be instituted, between Midsomer

Midsomer Norton signalbox and greenhouse (J F Rimmer)

Norton and Bath. This was done and single line working was instituted, which meant that all facing points had to be secured when required, a somewhat lengthy job for each train that could be run.

The roads to Bath being blocked, no cars or buses could travel and the news that a train was running meant that we were crowded with people wanting to get to Bath to work. Even so some passengers grumbled at having to wait while the points were secured. All went to work and all returned safely. I do not recollect one letter or word of appreciation from these one-off passengers after the line was cleared.

As the line was blocked beyond the station the wages for the staff beyond Midsomer Norton

Midsomer Norton up starting signal: porter changing lamp. Note the hanging basket on the signal ladder support (J F Rimmer)

had to be conveyed by Land Rover. Much has been published about engines sent to clear the line and getting lost over the Mendips. Signal wires were down which meant that the GPO service had to be used between Binegar and Midsomer Norton. An engine driver and fireman finding themselves marooned struggled through snowdrifts to an isolated farmhouse where they were able to get to a phone. I took the call saying they were safe.

Norman Rallison

I once had to do a time-and-motion study on the porters at Midsomer Norton station when there was a question of cutting staff. The best of it was that I lost the chap that I was watching at 8pm for an hour, he just disappeared. When I did meet up with him again I asked him where he had been, his reply was "I always go home after the down train for a cup of tea".

CHILCOMPTON

Chilcompton 19/5/65: looking towards Midsomer Norton. The water column is shrouded against frost (Colin Caddy)

Mike Ryall

I remember walking to work one day in 1963, it was 2:30am on a very cold Monday. I passed a house where the upstairs window was slightly open, I could hear this lucky beggar snoring his head off; it was then that I thought – with the snowflakes falling as big as two bob bits – that I must be mad going to work in this.

I was booked for the 3.30am goods to Evercreech Junction, you signed on at 3am, my driver was Len England. We left Bath Junction a few minutes late, we was told that the 2.40am Mail had gone through the section with an engine coupled in front with a snow plough attached. We got as far as Radstock station whereupon I went up to the signalbox to carry out Rule 55 and after about an hour we were told that we could go. By the time we had reached Chilcompton, the wind was blowing a gale and what with the snow it was getting pretty foul. We went through Chilcompton up a slight gradient under a road bridge and straight into a 15ft snowdrift, we stopped there for about an hour, during which time we were joined by the guard who was looking like the abominable snowman, poor chap. He had a warm and thawed out a bit and walked back to Chilcompton, which was about a half a mile, where arrangements were made to pull us back to where we detached our train into a siding and then proceeded back to Radstock where we took on water as the tender was nearly dry. I believe the line was blocked for several days because of heavy snowdrifts.

BINEGAR

Len Hardee

I remember when I went into the No 1 Link as a fireman on the S&D: I was teamed up with driver Bert Jones who I stayed with for five years. He was a good pal on and off duty. He used to take mutual improvement classes on Sunday mornings at Templecombe. This was a great help for me when I finally went in for my driver's exam. When we were waiting in the sidings or had any time to spare he would go around the engine and take me through the rules.

It was with Bert that I recall quite a frightening experience. It was in 1955: we were double-headed on the "Pines Express" from Evercreech Junction to Bath. We were on the leading engine which was a LMS class 2 and behind us was a class 5. We had 10 coaches on. We were travelling at about 60mph in the vicinity of Binegar when there was a loud bang: one of the top windows on the class 2 cab had shattered. We both thought a brick had come through. After we had composed ourselves from the shock there on the floor of the footplate was a cock pheasant. We both had a chuckle, I picked it up and put it into our food box. When we got to Bath we saw the fitter about putting a new window in. We explained what had happened. Once he had discovered what had caused the window to shatter he informed us that the pheasant was British Railways property. Bert soon put him right about whose pheasant it was. Two days later after it had been hanging in Bert's kitchen we shared it out.

Norman Rallison

In the 1950s I used to carry out relief signalling duties at Binegar. At this station there was quite a lot of calf traffic to Scotland, I recall one day Norman Down, the stationmaster, found his dog missing. He had everybody looking for it but it could not be found. The story got around that Binegar porter Joe Boucher had put it by mistake into the horse box that was used to transport the cattle. Everybody began to think that maybe this had happened until the dog turned up at the station later on. The poor bloke had his leg pulled for ages after this incident.

Binegar: 3F No 47557 with the driver enjoying sandwiches whilst waiting for the road – partial cleaning of the BR emblem and number give good effect (J F Rimmer)

Gordon Hatcher

In September 1956 I appeared in the making of the British Railways instructional film "Single Line Working" using two S&D stations, Shepton Mallet (which for the film purposes was called "Averton Hammer") and Binegar (which was named "Boiland"). It took three Sundays to make. My father Art Hatcher was also involved. On one Sunday he was driving BR Standard class 5 No 73047 with empty coaching stock. Other footplate crew that I remember were Jack Hix driving a BR Standard class 4 and Lou Long on a 7F No 53810 who was pulling an empty freight, I was on the banking engine 3F No 43194 my driver was Fritz Lawrence. I remember driver Percy Hobbs and Binegar stationmaster Norman Down also appeared in this film. It was great fun to be involved especially to see yourself on film later.

Binegar signalbox: 3F No 47557 having banked a freight train. The crew converse with the signalman before returning to Radstock (J F Rimmer)

MASBURY

Max Shore

As a junior porter in the war years one of my jobs was to clean and fill the up distant signal at Masbury, which could be quite a job. When the Americans came to Masbury things changed. They modified some eight jerry cans with small pouring spouts and filled them up with kerosene and secreted them away within 20 yards of each signal. This certainly made life a lot easier, especially when walking from Shepton Mallet station with a large container of oil. The Americans were very helpful and life became much easier. There were some occasions when I was taken across the fields by jeep to my signals. The Americans used to like our cider. I remember a driver Jimmy Lindsay who came from West Pennard to Shepton Mallet once a week in his 6-ton truck. He would meet the Americans at the station where he would exchange this rough genuine farmhouse cider for tobacco, cigarettes and chocolate. It was swiftly put on the jeeps and brought back to Masbury.

The Americans also used Masbury station to unload hundreds of thousands of jerry cans which were later filled with fuel from large tankers which came by the train load. The petrol dump stretched from Masbury to Thrupe and took some 18 months to build up, but when D-day arrived it was cleared in days.

I enjoyed my portering days at Masbury. There was only one other permanent resident there which was the signalman Harry Holbey.

Norman Rallison

One day sticks in my mind, it was on Sunday the 30th December 1962, snow was coming down hard. I was on duty at Masbury signalbox. Before I left at 4.30pm I told control at Bath that the snow plough should have run through. Nothing happened.

On the Monday I should have taken duty up at Stean Bow crossing. Around that time I was living near Cole station. I walked the line from Cole to Evercreech Junction box as the roads were blocked with snow. The snow was up to my knees in some places. I was hoping to pick up the 6am goods and ride on the engine up to the crossing, but nothing came through. I returned and stayed at Evercreech Junction box all day, clearing points. The next day and the rest of the week I was at Shepton Mallet, again clearing points and pilot working, this particular week I was putting in 16-hour days.

Masbury Station 1963: the signalbox which seems freshly painted with sidings still in use. Note the Bond Minicar at the rear (Colin Caddy)

WINSOR HILL

Mike Ryall

A mate of mine was working on the last up passenger from Templecombe, approaching Winsor Hill tunnel. He had put the shovel into the tender for some coal. On drawing it back out, there sat an owl looking at him with great big eyes. It nearly frightened him to death! He put him in a bucket with some newspaper and brought him back to Bath and then let him go.

SHEPTON MALLET

Gordon Hatcher

When I was a fireman at Branksome I remember working with driver Jim Tranter. We were taking the "Pines Express" from Bournemouth West to Bath. The engine was a Black 5 and we had 12 coaches on. I was on the footplate when Jim got on board with a big basket. "What's in there?" I said. "My racing pigeons" he replied. When we stopped at Shepton Mallet he got the basket out and released these pigeons, where I gather his wife timed them back to his loft at Branksome.

Frank Staddon

I remember Friday 1st February 1946. The 10.30pm freight train passed over Shepton Mallet viaduct. After the train had passed over the viaduct one side of it collapsed. On the Saturday morning driver Moore and myself worked a three coach set to Shepton Mallet and back to Bath. I shall never forget the eerie feeling passing over the viaduct and looking straight down into the street below with loose ballast still falling. Full marks to the inspector who passed the single line safe to travel over.

Cliff Smith

In the early 1950's I recall working the 5.00am goods from Bath to Evercreech. As we left Shepton Mallet the crew on a train coming up from Evercreech called out as we passed "There's a cow on the line". We kept our eyes open for this cow. It was very dark at the time. We at last saw it in front of us. My driver went as slow as he could while I ran in front trying to chase it off the line, but instead the cow stayed on the line walking in front of the train. This went on for quite a while. Dawn was now breaking and I now saw I had been chasing a bull! I got back on the loco a bit quick. Fortunately the bull went down the bank on its own accord.

Mike Ryall

Just before closure in early 1966 I had a job with driver Ben Ford to take two light engines coupled together to Templecombe and bring back a empty pigeon special. On arriving at Templecombe upper siding we were coupled up to our train. The guard came up and said "You have got 22 coaches on, driver, and 582 tons". When I heard this I nearly collapsed. Considering that the maximum load was 475 tons for a double-header, you can appreciate what a job this was. I believe that this was the largest train over the S&D during peace time.

Our locomotive was a 0-6-0 Midland class 4 No 44558 which was well known to be a poor steamer. Assisting us was a Standard 5 with driver Bill Rawles on the footplate. We arrived at Evercreech Junction where we had a banker. Coming out of Evercreech you're going into gradients of up to 1:50 to the top of Masbury Summit, with a drop in Shepton Mallet half way up. We arrived over the summit with ¾ of a glass of water, the needle just behind the red mark on the steam gauge. This was one of my hardest firing turns, a real achievement against all the odds. I've never worked so hard in my life and when Ben got off the driver's seat and wiped his brow with his handkerchief and said "I've really worked hard on this trip" I had to laugh.

Max Shore

I started work at Charlton Road, Shepton Mallet, as a junior porter in April 1943. I was only 14 years of age. All my workmates were over the age of 65 and being a strapping young lad I did the majority of the manual work. My hours were 8am to 6pm and my wage was 15 shillings a week.

I was introduced to all aspects of life and work at the station. One of my main tasks was fetching five quarts of rough cider every morning for consumption at break time (10.45am) for the staff. I was soon introduced to cleaning signal lamps, my colleagues being a bit on the old side didn't want to walk the distance. This was not too bad at Shepton as we had a spare lamp and you could clean them in the lamp shed, but Winsor Hill and Masbury were extremely difficult. You walked from Shepton carrying a large container of oil. This became heavy

Top: Shepton Mallet signalbox, 1960s. Bottom: general view looking north. The signal is off and passengers are waiting so the stopping train is due soon (J F Rimmer)

after a couple of miles, not a pleasant walk in the cold winter months. When reaching Winsor Hill tunnel I was always a bit scared when entering, especially in the down tunnel. It was very dark and you couldn't see round the corner; first indication of a train coming was a whistle when it entered the tunnel. You had seconds to get yourself up against the wall before the train was on you. I only used this route a couple of times. I soon reverted to the up tunnel where you could see right through to the other end. Situated here was one of the tallest signals and what a job it was! You had to climb the signal retrieve the lamp, climb down then find a sheltered spot, clean the lamp, put fresh oil in it and re-light, climb back up and check that it was still alight. In the winter months on a wet and windy day it was not uncommon to use up a box of matches and climb up and down 15 to 20 times before being successful. After completing this signal at Winsor Hill I carried on to the up distant at Masbury, which was a mile away. Once I had attended to the signal I used to try and get a lift back to Shepton on the slow goods train. The drivers were always looking out for you, mind you they were still going a speed, but at 15 years of age I use to run like hell and jump on the guards van. While I was at Shepton Mallet I became an expert at washing out cattle trucks. We had an unending procession of pigs for the bacon factory and because of a shortage of trucks they had to be turned around in a day. The record was 32 in a day. Saturdays at Shepton was very hectic; the 10.56am down from Bath would disgorge anything from up to 200 passengers. They were not for Shepton: they would cross over and book for the "Pines". Evidently you could never get on at Bath. When eventually the "Pines" arrived, anything up to an hour late, one would push and cram people into the carriages and on some occasions people were left behind. Often the "Pines" pulled up outside the goods shed (prior to the up platform) and call for the shunting engine for assistance to Binegar. In the opposite direction from Bath the 5.28pm Shepton was in the winter very often up to three hours late. It got to the stage that if they had a loco and a couple of coaches at Bath they would run a local to Evercreech Junction.

One day after D-day the prison at Shepton Mallet occupied by the Americans was emptied. All the prisoners came to the station (some 400 of them), all handcuffed in one long line. There were machine guns around the station perimeter and on the footbridge. The special troop train arranged to take them to the coast was some 40 minutes late. This caused much concern with all the guards. When the train arrived they were put in the coaches handcuffed in fours. This was 6.15am and we were on overtime to get them away. We were called back at 10.30pm the same day to unload the same train; the weather was too bad in the channel and they couldn't embark. The whole exercise was repeated two days later and they did not return.

One famous incident that I recall was when walking back from signalling duties from Winsor Hill on a cold, wet, windy Friday. As I was so wet I decided that when I reached the Waterloo Road Viaduct I would take shelter. The bridge had been scaffolded to enable repairs to take place. Underneath one of the centre spans was Tom Corbin, a mason who was pointing the bricks with cement, we had a cigarette and a chat, a train passed over the viaduct and some of the cement came out. I remarked on the subject to Tom only to be told "If it wasn't safe, son, I would not be here". Seven hours later at 10.55pm on 1st February 1946 the bridge collapsed.

Archie Gunning
An incident which I remembered was in 1946 when I was driving the 5.00pm goods train for Poole.

After we had stopped at Evercreech Junction we had to change trains at Templecombe goods yard and Templecombe men took the train further on. We had to carry out some shunting at Evercreech to make up the train to Bath, then had to wait some time before we were booked to go. We had some supper on our engine. Whilst we were eating the shunter's cabin bell started to ring. The head shunter came out and told us that we were not going anywhere; Bath Road

Viaduct at Shepton Mallet had collapsed at 10.55pm on the up line and we could not get home. The stationmaster came up to the yard and told us to take the engine back to Templecombe shed. We caught a train from there to Salisbury and onto Bath Spa. It was very late when we got home to the loco shed and booked off. We were lucky because we could have been travelling on the viaduct when it collapsed.

EVERCREECH NEW STATION

Edna Simms

I was a booking office clerk at Evercreech New station. It was in 1940 and World War Two had been underway for a few months. My job consisted of issuing tickets, informing local companies of truck consignments, preparing books for audit and answering queries from the general public. Being wartime conditions there was lots of enquiries regarding the running of trains. We always made sure that we gave as much help as possible to the public, and to the various companies around Evercreech.

Evercreech New: a view looking north showing LSWR signals and the disused kiln
(J F Rimmer)

In those days there were many search light batteries stationed around Evercreech and on the high slopes and hills of Batcombe, Westcombe and Alham. Sometimes our telephone would ring from the soldiers who manned the batteries. They would inform us that they were going on leave and hoped to catch the next train. They would borrow a bicycle and ask us to hold the train if they didn't arrive in time. Well you can imagine, can't you, what to do for the best when the train arrived, and no soldier? We would have a quick word with the guard. Most of them on the S&D were helpful and kind. I would watch the goods yard entrance road and somebody else would watch the little path which ran into the passenger entrance, the bicycle would be quickly abandoned, the gate held open, and usually the soldier jumped on the train and gave a wave from the carriage as it steamed out of Evercreech.

In those days of food rationing we all seemed to be black marketeers, I had one or two friends who helped the food situation. I remember one very dark and frosty morning when I left my home at Castle Cary, which was approximately five miles from Evercreech. On my bicycle I had half a dozen freshly caught rabbits hanging on my handlebars, how I managed to cycle that distance with my cargo I don't know. I used to barter the rabbits with the Americans who were stationed there for food items that we never had.

I had one very lucky escape at Evercreech New station. We suddenly heard this German plane come over and drop his bombs at Prestleigh. I had opened the waiting room door to go onto the platform when one of the porters gave me a backward push. I landed on the waiting room floor with him falling on top of me. One of the German planes turned towards the station and machine gunned right through the station, I was very lucky that I was thrown back by the porter.

In April 1942 I married Ted Simms, whose family had a long tradition of working on the Somerset and Dorset Railway. Ted was a signalman at Evercreech as was his father; his uncle Jack Simms was a passenger guard at Bath Green Park, and there was my husband's sister Betty Cox (née Simms) who was a porteress at Evercreech Junction.

Betty was the first girl to be employed as a porteress. Other girls there at the time were Betty Spiller, Betty Lambert and Joyce Reakes.

Betty related to me one day about when the Italian prisoners of war were brought daily by coach to work in the sidings. She remembered looking on with envy as they cooked their breakfast of bacon, while they sat down and ate their bread and marg. One person I must mention was the stationmaster who was at Evercreech New during my employment there, his name was Bob Hayes. He came from West Pennard station on the Evercreech to Burnham-on-Sea branch line. He tried to keep all his staff happy through these difficult years, which he succeeded in doing. Other colleagues I worked with were Emily Poole who was also a clerk, Fred Ward the drayman, porters Walter Field, Jack Cox, Charles Hartnell and Ted Stoneman, lengthmen Tom Billing, Alf Clarke and Reg Lucas.

After all these years I still remember all of them. The period of my employment on the S&D was a very happy and interesting time. Everyone was prepared to help one another and we seemed to still keep in touch with many of the inhabitants of Evercreech and the business people.

One thing I must say, and this is having worked on this most famous railway: we are so surprised when people find out this in conversation with us, we then have to answer so many questions.

EVERCREECH JUNCTION

Arthur King

The funniest story I can remember happened one night when I was on the 7.15pm freight from Bath to Templecombe. We were approaching Lamyatt level crossing after leaving Evercreech Junction, the crossing signal was against us (which was very unusual as it was hardly used at night) and we had almost stopped when it was pulled off but the crossing keeper was stopping us on the crossing with his hand lamp. We stopped and he handed us up a sack bag. In it was six rabbits he had caught. He said would we drop him off a bit of coal on the way back as he had none of his allowance left. When we arrived at Templecombe I got on the tender to throw the coal at the back, forward for our return journey to Bath. While I was doing this I came across a very large lump of coal about four foot long. I thought this would do for the crossing keeper so I put it on the side of the tender to push off at the crossing. We had to run tender first from Templecombe to Evercreech Junction. Getting near to the crossing I climbed onto the tender and stood the lump of coal up on its end and pushed it off at the keeper's cottage. It went through his fence and crashed into his front door, breaking it down. The next night he stopped us again and said "Next time I want some coal don't try and put it in my firegrate". He had a new door fitted and told the company that a lump of coal had fell off a passing train during the night and caused the damage.

Tony Axford

One dark night in the 1960's my driver Reg and myself were on a Midland class 2 tank engine, we were going light engine tender first from Evercreech Junction to Templecombe. Reg remarked that we had better get a move on as the last down passenger from Bath Green Park was not far behind us. These little engines used to ride well and we were really going at some speed. We came upon the tall warning signal south of Evercreech Junction this was supposed to caution you if the next crossing was against the train. It was on amber as we rushed past. Nobody took too much notice of this signal as it was always on caution. This crossing was only a quiet farm track as far as I can recall. We were really motoring when we approached the crossing. Suddenly I could just make out a white shape in the darkness in front of us and I could see no lamps. I said to Reg something to the effect that the gates were across the track. Reg slammed on the brakes and started to put the engine in forward gear. There was an almighty crash. I remember seeing large pieces of white gate timbers flying past the cab and it almost seemed to be happening in slow motion. We eventually stopped some way down the line and thankfully we were still on the track. Reg instructed me to carry out a protection procedure. I walked back through the rubble in the pitch darkness and placed detonators on the track to protect us from the next down.

At the enquiry the relief gate keeper was supposed to have said that the first thing he did was to feel the gate lamps which were still hot. What presence of mind when one minute you are in the gatekeeper's house watching the Clay v Liston fight on television and the next you are looking at two very large crossing gates that have just been obliterated right outside the living room window!

Charles Vaughan

When I joined the S&D in 1943, war was in its fourth year. I lived about three miles from Evercreech Junction where I worked as a shunter on three shifts. I enjoyed the job but I must admit one occasion sticks in my mind. It was in the winter of 1963. Normally it only took me 20 minutes to cycle to work, but the beginning of January snow was falling at an alarming rate. I remember it taking me four hours to get to work; the snow was so high that cars were completely covered in and I was actually walking on top of them with my bicycle. This went on for days but on the railway you carried on: it was your job.

One of these mornings one of the porters had not turned up for work. The stationmaster became worried and phoned his home, and found out that he had left for work. Myself and another chap was sent out to find him. We battled across fields in the deep snow in the direction of his home. Unfortunately we found Joe Kemp frozen to death in the snow. We laid him on a gate and struggled back with him. Everybody at Evercreech was deeply distressed and our hearts went out to his family.

I had some happy and sad times on the S&D. I enjoyed the job being the head shunter. There was always a lot of activity at Evercreech, and the shunters' cabin was well known for its tea for the visiting footplate crews who came to the junction.

I worked for three stationmasters: Mr Pike, Mr Stowe and Mr Newman. At 88 years of age I would still love to do the job now.

Evercreech Junction: above – fireman Bruce Briant is pulling down coal on the tender of 4F No 44558, the pilot an unknown 7F (B Briant collection). Below is a view from the overbridge with mailsacks being transferred from down to up platform to await a train (J F Rimmer)

Gordon Hatcher

One journey we used to make from Templecombe was a freight train called "The Tripper". We used mostly 7Fs. We would go out empty from the upper yard to Evercreech Junction in the morning and bring back a loaded one; anything from coal to barrels of beer from Burton-on-Trent which used to go to Devonport. You could carry this out three times for a day's work.

Talking about Evercreech, it was in 1945, VJ Day. I was firing the 7pm passenger train out of Bath. We worked it as far as Templecombe; my driver was Bill Goddard. We stopped at Evercreech to top up with water. We put the pipe in and turned the water on. Whilst we were doing this a porter informed us that as it was VJ Day: there was a free barrel of beer at The Railway Hotel for railwaymen, so we shot across the road for a couple of pints. When we came back Evercreech Junction station was flooding. I'd left the water on, and the tender was overflowing.

COLE

Gerald Trowbridge

One day I was invited to have a ride on the footplate of a Bulldog class 3F by driver Den Norris. I was a junior porter at the time. After the ride I decided it was a footplate life for me, so I transferred to Templecombe where I became a cleaner and progressed to a fireman sometime later. I thoroughly enjoyed firing to the old drivers. They were real characters.

My first firing turn on a passenger train was to driver "Doctor" Montague. They called him doctor because of the doctor's bag he carried around with him. We were on a Black 5 4-6-0 No 5056, my first time on this class of engine. I thought my dreams had come true, it was wonderful. I had worked mostly on 2Ps so to climb aboard and see the spacious cab with its look of sheer power was quite daunting. The footplate floor was clean and the controls were shining; I felt I was firing on the Rolls Royce of engines.

Another driver that I remember was George Williams, he liked his breakfast of bacon and eggs on the shovel, which I had previously cleaned and scalded for him. I used to warm a pork pie on the clack box for myself and with a can of tea it was a good start to the day.

One memorable journey I recall was on a 3F. We used to go light engine to Evercreech to assist goods trains up the bank to Masbury. This particular driver used to stop just outside Cole. There was a cutting there with lots of rabbits running around. He would pull out this 12-bore shotgun which he had leaning up against the gear change and would then start popping away at these rabbits. He used to say "Gerald when they fall down you get off the footplate and go and fetch them". He was not a very good shot and I didn't have to get off the footplate too much. There was never a dull moment with him, he enjoyed his scrumpy and always carried a pint bottle of this around with him. He was also a part time bookmaker, placing bets on the horses for everybody. He certainly introduced me to life and was always very helpful on the footplate.

Norman Rallison

Quaint goings-on that I recall was when the 8.15am school train from Templecombe arrived at Cole. After the children had got off the crew of the engine would go to Mrs Box the crossing keeper at Bruton Road crossing and supply her with hot water from the engine for her washing. Also the 12.00 goods from Evercreech used to bring her churns of water and a good supply of coal. In the 1950s there was no water or electricity laid on at the crossings.

Percy Hobbs

I was working with a driver called Jack Hix; we were on a class 7. We brought a large bag of peat from Evercreech Junction downside to Cole for a well known shunter called "Mutton". He wanted it for his spring plants. Jack and I both enjoyed a joke: we picked up pieces of brick arch around the down sidings, and stuffed them into this bag of peat. Also I put the injector on and slackened the pipe nozzle into the bag of peat, and gave it a good soaking. Well, when we arrived at Cole the porter was there waiting for us with this old barrow. We got alongside him, and pushed this bag of peat off the side of the engine. It hit the barrow and broke it clean in half. We laughed about this for weeks, as did "Mutton" the shunter. Fortunately the authorities did not hear about this incident, otherwise there would have been some explaining to do.

Cole Station looking south: the standard rose looks healthy; the sagging roof of the up platform shelter seems sad (J F Rimmer)

WINCANTON

Fred Lester

Being a district relief clerk on the S&D in the 1950's took me to many stations and I also met quite a few stationmasters. It is difficult to describe the respect accorded to stationmasters in those days: no first name familiarity and ideas of equality; they were universally addressed as Sir and this was the same in the local community. I quickly recognized the importance of building good relationships because it depended on their tolerance whether I could work to suit the train times and get home most nights.

One such stationmaster at Wincanton was Charlie Lethbridge, a mild-mannered gentleman in the full meaning of the word. In the course of the years that followed I probably spent more time at Wincanton than any other station. This was a station literally in the shadow of the huge Cow and Gate milk factory. There was the usual small market town trade but milk tanks and baby food products sent country-wide dominated the office work in a way unlike other places except perhaps Bason Bridge, which also served a milk factory.

Ron Gray

My worst experience as a driver was when working the fastest train of the day on the S&D, even faster than the "Pines Express". It was the 9.40am Bath to Bournemouth and my fireman was Ron Merchant. You didn't go into Templecombe upper, you stopped only at Evercreech Junction and Broadstone. We had just gone through Wincanton. We had a speedometer on this Black 5 and we had reached 90mph. On looking ahead I saw this boy on the track waving his coat frantically. I immediately shut down the regulator and slammed the brakes on. When we did stop we were just a few yards past Shepton Montague. There was a farm crossing with a five-bar gate and there was no signal there. A very heavy farm van had broken down and his axle had sheared off. The obstruction was on our line. We only had 6 coaches on but it was packed with holidaymakers. I'm not exaggerating in saying we actually stopped a matter of yards from this vehicle.

We couldn't thank this boy enough, without his bravery we would have been involved in a very serious accident. We got on the phone and the permanent way men and some farm labourers came and cleared the obstruction. We then continued our journey, rather shaken. A few days later I spoke to the stationmaster at Wincanton and asked whether the railway had done anything to thank or reward this boy; as far as I know they never did. He was a very brave lad, and one I shall never forget. He saved many lives that day.

Norman Rallison

When I first went to Wincanton, on race days the platforms would be filled with people going to and from the races, and there would be at least a dozen horse boxes in the yard.

I remember on one occasion I was on duty at Wincanton. It was a Saturday night and the last passenger train had pulled in. This young couple got off the train. They had just got married and they were on their honeymoon. They came over to the signalbox and asked when the next train to Bournemouth was due. I replied "Monday morning, 8.45am". After the sudden shock they explained that they had come down from Bath and instead of keeping on the train they had got out at Templecombe for some refreshments. When they came back onto the platform they got into the wrong part of the train. The train they came down on was the 7pm Bath to Bournemouth and the 6.40pm Bournemouth to Bath joined up at Templecombe No 2. They both left the same station together, when it got to Templecombe No 2, they split and went their different ways. To try and help them I stopped the 9pm Bath to Poole goods, saw the guard and got them on board. When I saw the guard again he said "I bet they will remember their first night together, we had to shunt at every station going down to Poole".

PARK LANE CROSSING

Joan Fisher

Joan Fisher at Park Lane Crossing 1940

When we moved to Templecombe we found it very difficult to find a house. There was a vacancy for a crossing keeper at Park Lane crossing, so we took that and my mother became the keeper. Park Lane was the second crossing between Templecombe and Henstridge, the other being Common Lane: that was manned by Mr. Elkins. When I moved into the house it was three months after my mother and father had already moved in as I was working at Bath. I remember dad met me at the station and said it was a nice little cottage. When I woke up the next morning it was not what I expected: candle lights, Tilley lamps, and a well for water. But this was all we could get. I stayed there for 11 years. Early mornings when the Summer Specials roared by on their way to Bournemouth, we were greeted by the clunk, clunk, of coal thrown off the footplate into our yard, mostly by the Bath crews. I remember drivers Ralph Holden and a driver called Lee. The favourite one with the coal was good old Johnny Walker, he always made sure that we had plenty of coal.

We used to open the crossing gates for Miss Guest's hounds from Inwood House Henstridge. They were part of the Blackmoor Hunt and if you were quick enough she would give you 2/6d.

The farmers with the hay-making would be frequent visitors in the summer, crossing the line as late as midnight. With the backdrop of a brilliant red sky in the distance, it was a lovely setting. Funny enough in those days it always seemed much lighter at night.

I remember Maurice Gawler who was a ganger: he walked the line from Stalbridge to Templecombe most days, come rain or shine. If it was a hot day he would stop at the crossing for a glass of our lovely cold water from the well. Other plate-layers that I remember were Fred Foot and Bert Cluett. They worked hard through all kinds of weather. Most of them lived into their 80s and 90s.

In fact I was actually employed on the S&D for two weeks as a crossing keeper. Mr Sealy the controller from Bath came down to see me and check that everything was alright. There were no signals at Park Lane. Early mornings were very busy, especially in the war years with the Americans coming through. About 20 trains used to come through each day. In the summer months there was more with all the specials running through. We used to have the "Pines Express" tearing through. You got a toot on the whistle and a friendly wave from the crew: that used to make my day.

My father was also in the Home Guard at Templecombe and was called out on many a job. I remember in the war visiting some friends in Templecombe when the sirens came on, I hurriedly made my way to the crossing as bombs were coming down over Templecombe – quite a frightening feeling. Unfortunately my father passed away while still in service in 1959. He had been on the S&D for 39 years. It was his life. He really enjoyed it, the friendliness of many colleagues, people like guards Dickie Bird, Reg Brewer, Paddy Smythe, and one in particular (from Bournemouth) was Alf Metcalf.

Also there were drivers Charlie King, Ronald Andrews and Midford signalman Percy Savage. They were all S&D men through and through, happy memories for him and me.

Being brought up on the S&D gave me the feeling I was always part of this beautiful old country railway. I left the crossing in 1952 and got married, to an S&D man of course: Fred Fisher, who I met whilst watching a football match with my father at Henstridge. He was a driver at Templecombe.

TEMPLECOMBE

Percy Hobbs

I was a fireman at Templecombe in the Second World War, I remember joining the Railway Home Guard. We were a bit of a ragtag bunch at the beginning. All we had between us was two single bore shotguns to guard our depot with. Eventually we were issued with American rifles and one of these nearly caused a serious accident. Our shed foreman Bernard Dyer and his under foreman Ken Anderson were examining one of these rifles in the office when it suddenly went off. The bullet ricocheted off the fireplace and hit Mr Anderson in the leg. He gave a good old yelp and was rushed to hospital. Fortunately it was not serious. I must admit all the Home Guard lads had a little chuckle about this.

I recall there was lots of enemy aircraft over the Templecombe area and on one occasion a single German plane on the way back from Yeovil came down towards the depot and put a couple of bullets through the smokebox of a "King Arthur". We heard later that this plane was shot down over Andover.

Another time we were at the shed about 7pm one evening when German planes came over. We all darted under the turntable. The bombs came down near Combe Throop Lane. When the bombing had finished we all got out and stood around the turntable when suddenly we heard faint cries for help. We rushed over to the shed from where the noise was coming. On reaching the shed we could tell it was coming from the sand bin. This bin was a big round iron barrel shape. It stood about 10ft tall. The shed labourer Fred Chant was in it. It appears that Fred was emptying sand bags from above when the bombs went off. He fell into the bin and was swamped in sand and could not get out.

We all had a good laugh, we pulled him out unhurt and some of the names he was calling Adolf Hitler are unprintable.

At Templecombe Upper we had an ambulance train berthed in the down sidings. It had an LNER engine which was fitted with Westinghouse brakes. It was kept coaled up ready to be called out at a moment's notice. There was always a crew on standby that went out with this train wherever it was sent, which was usually a few days at a time.

One lasting memory of the war years was when we were at Evercreech Junction sidings in the shunters' lobby. From here you could see a train coming out of the cutting from Shepton Mallet down over Prestleigh. You could see the engine wheels spitting out fire from the braking – it was like a giant catherine wheel. It was the same when the guards van brake came on; just a red hot glow. It was an unbelievable sight and how the Germans never spotted this we never knew.

Bill Harford

I was a driver at Branksome in the 1950s and I remember one Saturday night I was taking the milk train from Templecombe to Bailey Gate and then light engine to Branksome shed. We didn't leave Templecombe until 11pm which was after the last passenger train had left. We were just about to leave when the station foreman rushed over and asked me if I could give a young nurse who was still in her uniform a lift to Poole. She was stranded at Templecombe after arriving late from Exeter. I readily agreed but there was one problem: we had no guards van and just two milk tanks behind us. We overcame this problem by taking a chair out of the waiting room and putting it on the footplate of the 4F loco. The nurse climbed aboard, sat on the chair and we made our way to Poole. On the journey she enjoyed a can of tea with us and we were only too pleased to help her out: that was what the S&D was all about.

Percy Hobbs

It was in the 1950's that I started to do some driving turns. In 1955 I became a registered driver at Templecombe. I remember it well, as it was the year of the ASLEFF strike.

My favourite engines on the S&D were the Black 5s: they had that little bit extra over the other classes. But one of the nicest engines that I drove was the West Country Pacific No 34040 "Crewkerne". On this occasion in the late 1950s, I took her out with fireman Derek Howcutt. It was the 3.30pm goods from Poole. She had just come out of the shop and she looked a picture. It was a pleasure to drive her that day.

One incident that comes to mind was when I was driving 9F No 92220 *Evening Star*. It was in the early 1960s. Dick Issacs was my fireman. We had picked her up from Templecombe at 5.30pm and we had 8 carriages on. Ivo Peters the well known photographer was chasing us that summer's day, and what a day it was. The fireman who had brought her up from Bournemouth had left the footplate nice and clean for us, but when we opened the firebox it was black. By the time we had got to the top of Evercreech New, I was right out and very nearly right down. We stirred and poked the fire with the irons. We tried everything to help get it going, but we couldn't get it to burn right through until we were almost up to Masbury. How we got to our destination I'll never know. From when we picked it up from Templecombe and arrived at Bath, we never put any coal on at all, and of course Ivo was following our journey with interest. He took various pictures of us on that day over the Mendips, I saw him a couple of weeks later and he asked me what had happened. I explained that we had inherited a rather full firebox at Templecombe, which made the journey extremely difficult.

I remember the bad winter of 1963 at Templecombe. Notices were posted, telling us drivers to make sure that sufficient coal was thrown off at all water columns where there were fires. Also the fires were to be poked out and filled with fresh coal. This was carried out everywhere. There was also baskets of fires in all walkways in the shed. They were beside the injectors on all engines. The fitters were also kept busy de-icing the frozen injectors.

I remember at Evercreech Junction downside, some box vans were completely buried for several days, and also engines were buried where they had stopped in the vicinity of Winsor Hill. The snow plough had bumped into them whilst they were clearing the snow.

Mike Baker

I was the last person to start work on the Somerset and Dorset Railway at Templecombe loco depot. It was in May 1965. I started as a cleaner and within two days, because there was a shortage of firemen, I was sent to firing school at Bath, and duly passed out as a fireman.

During my short period of cleaning I remember cleaning up BR Standard 4 2-6-4T No 80043. I used to travel on the footplate when I went to firing school. We caught the 7am Templecombe to Bath. The loco rostered for the first day to firing school was good old 80043 so we had a nice clean engine that week.

I was passed for firing by driver Pat Evans, who also used to run mutual improvement classes, and I later became his fireman. One of the worst turns I remember was the 12.05 Templecombe to Bath. The loco was normally a Bournemouth engine, BR class 4 2-6-0. The worst of the class was 76013 (we called it unlucky 13) – the tubes were usually blocked. Talk about hard graft! You never stopped shovelling: every time you looked at the pressure gauge it was sinking rapidly, not helped by poor quality coal. Going through your mind was "are we going to make it to the top?". This is one turn that you actually sweated blood. Making it to the top of Masbury was a great relief.

On one occasion on this turn I was with driver Arthur Hatcher. He was normally in the shunting link, I presume due to his seemingly great age. At that time he was very seldom seen on the main line. We had the usual rough class 4, but Arthur handled the loco perfectly. We kept good time and must have nearly been in mid gear going up to Masbury much to the disgust of some enthusiasts with tape recorders as the loco was going very quietly. We went over the top with

Templecombe 1958: Walter Webb at the controls of the steam crane used for lifting coal tubs into loco tender (collection D Howcutt)

the safety valve lifting and plenty of water in the boiler; this was the only time I had a good trip on the 12.05 to Bath.

A turn I enjoyed was the 7am Templecombe to Bath returning with the 9.55am semi-fast, where we were relieved by another Templecombe crew who would take it on to Bournemouth. The usual loco on the up run was a BR Standard class 4 2-6-4 with a class 5 on the return run. Both classes of loco were excellent to work, comfortable and good steamers. The class 5s would perform so well that I remember on one occasion we had an unusually heavy load due to some vans attached to the train. On leaving Radstock the exhaust steam injector was put on and left on until we reached Masbury Summit, also using the live steam injector as required. The needle of the steam pressure gauge was on the line all the time and every time the driver closed the regulator the safety valves lifted instantly.

It was on this turn one day on the down run I lost the shovel at Bath Junction. I had just collected the tablet for the single line section to Midford and as I turned to show it to the driver I saw the shovel disappear over the right hand side, I shouted to my driver who stopped the train immediately. I then had to run back some distance to find the shovel, a rather embarrassing incident.

George Skinner

I once lost a tablet on a trip to Bath on a Saturday morning in the summer. I put the tablet in the catcher at the distant signal for Templecombe lower (which was the practice) only to find it gone when we reached the signalbox. This of course was a serious problem. When we arrived at Bath we were met by a railway inspector who searched the footplate. The line that morning was brought to a standstill. There were very strict rules which apply to single line working. They found the tablet later that morning on the line bank, and also found that the engine catcher was faulty.

The job had its funny moments, I well remember when working a down train from Bath one afternoon. We had left Templecombe lower and as we came up to the road bridge we could not believe our eyes, for at the first crossing cottage (which by the way was very close to the track) a man was up a ladder working on the gutter of the cottage, with the base of the ladder on the track. The brake and whistle went on together, and you should have seen the speed of descent from a ladder in such circumstances! The ladder and the man just escaped in time. We did not report the incident as the crossing keeper would have got into trouble.

Gordon Hatcher

In the late 1940s another fireman Cyril Read and myself volunteered for the summer season working out of Branksome. I fired to Johnny Walker. There was never a dull moment; he was a lovely man to work with, a very good engineman, and had a great sense of humour. I remember going into the buffet at Templecombe with him. He was wearing this large overcoat. Johnny had this old motor car horn which he used to put under his arm inside his coat. We went in for a cup of tea; he could squeeze this horn with his arm, and what a noise! We both kept a straight face, the customers started to look around, everybody looked at each other... they couldn't see where the noise was coming from.

Another funny incident, or I thought it was at the time, but the person concerned didn't: Bill Goddard, a driver at Templecombe shed, came in for work one morning between 3am and 4am. He was on duty that time all week. The night chargeman asked him "What are you doing here?" and Bill replied "Booking on, of course". The chargeman started laughing and Bill said "What are you laughing at?" The chargeman said "It's your rest day today" so Bill had to turn around and go home, back to bed. It was quite some time before he lived that down.

 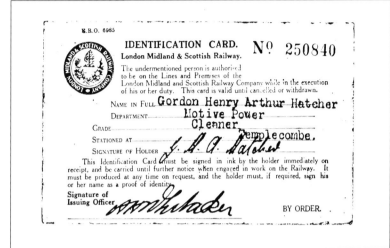

A job that I didn't look forward to in the winter months was the early turn out of Templecombe. I used to get out of a warm bed at 3am, cycle down to the depot, and if it was frosty or had been snowing you was frozen before you arrived. Then you had to prepare your engine which was nearly always a 7F.

You ran light to Evercreech Junction which was about 15 miles, tender first because the turntable at Templecombe was not big enough to turn those 7Fs. You would put your storm sheet up to try and protect yourself from the elements. I used to put my big overcoat on and a scarf around my ears, anything to keep warm. When you arrived at Evercreech you felt you'd already done a day's work. You were frozen. You went straight into the cabin where sometimes we'd enjoy a cup of tea with Charlie Vaughan, the shunter at Evercreech, who then helped us put the freight wagons onto our 7F, where we duly took it on to Poole.

It was through working on the S&D that I met my late lovely wife Anne. She lived at home with her parents, which was between Bournemouth West station and Branksome station. Their back garden backed onto the railway carriage siding. Opposite their house was a ground signal. The engines used to line up to go out onto the main line there. We had to go around the triangle to turn around. One day I stopped at the signal and I spotted this girl in her garden, I gave her a wave and she came down to the wooden fence, so I went over and had a chat, and that's how it started. We had a good 33 years of marriage. After a while Anne could tell the sound of the S&D engines from the Southern engines. I was always grateful to the S&D for bringing us together. I finished at Templecombe in 1958 and moved on to Bournemouth Central. I continued firing and driving there.

Fred Fisher

I have some lovely memories. I remember my first firing turn: the fireman had not turned up for duty for this particular trip and I was given the job. I could not believe it. It was on the "Pines Express" from No 2 Junction at Templecombe.

The driver was Walt Jeans. He helped me with the firing and we finished the job without a problem. I shall always treasure the memory of my first firing turn on the good old "Pines Express" with a first class driver who I fired to on many occasions.

I remember a driver Ron Spiller and myself testing a Southern Region engine class U1 Mogul 2-6-0 for possible use over the S&D for passenger work. We had to go down to Bournemouth Central and get the engine ready with inspector Jack Hookey who would be riding on the footplate with us.

We ran light engine to Bournemouth West and worked the 11.40 Sheffield train as far as Templecombe, on our way up we were going through Shillingstone around 60 to 70mph. Jack Hookey turned around and said to me "These engines will stick it okay, Fred", to which I replied "The engines might stick it Jack, but the poor old fireman won't". The coal on the footplate was bouncing up and down like hailstones with the bad vibrations. The U1 engines were eventually taken off from passenger work over the S&D.

Percy Hobbs

A driving job I used to enjoy in the late 1950s, was assisting the "Pines Express", from Evercreech to Bath. For this work we used 2Ps, one of the engines I remember was No 40569. We used to to get three hours at Bath waiting for the "Down Pines", then we would assist to Evercreech. From there we would go back to Templecombe light engine. That was a nice trip.

Talking about Templecombe days I remember a very funny story: it was in 1946; the shedmaster's name was Bernard Dyer. He always wore a bowler hat and called everybody "mee sonny". He was a fair man but wouldn't take any nonsense. Anyway a certain passed cleaner was late for duty, and Mr Dyer asked him why he was late. This passed cleaner gave him some back chat with some bad language mixed in. Mr Dyer was not impressed. Moving his bowler hat to the back of his head (you knew when he did this that he was not a happy man), he turned around and said "Now look here, mee sonny, now you go home, and when you go over Church Hill, you go into the Co-op and buy yourself a bar of carbolic soap, then go home and wash your mouth out. Stay home tomorrow and give it a good rinse, you come back the next day and I'll decide whether I will start you". Well after that every time we saw this passed cleaner at Bath or Bournemouth we used to ask him how he was off for carbolic soap.

Norman Rallison

All resident signalmen took great pride in the cleanliness of their boxes. The early turn man used to do the cleaning. At Templecombe No 2 the signalman used to take the train register book to the door for the engine men to sign Rule 55, rather than have them walk over the floor.

One night on duty at Common Lane crossing I was talking on the telephone to a signalman at Evercreech. As one knows, other signalmen can listen in to calls. This particular phone call was about gardening and sprout plants were mentioned. After we had finished talking I had a call from a crossing keeper at Bruton Road telling me he wouldn't mind some sprout plants. "Of course" I said. Near the crossing was a field of kale plants. I pulled some up and sent them to the crossing keeper as sprout plants. Later he told me these plants are growing well; he had given them some fertiliser and they were like trees, after that I never heard anything more about them "sprout" plants.

HENSTRIDGE

Henstridge (J F Rimmer)

Gordon Hatcher

Henstridge was a station that I remember well. It was on the borders of Somerset and Dorset. When I was a fireman I came through here quite a few times. We used to put off wagons of coal into the single line siding for the local coal merchant. You had to hand the electric tablet to the porter-cum-shunter so that he could insert it into a ground frame which enabled him to operate the points into the sidings. When you had finished the shunt he would close the points, withdraw the tablet and hand it back to you so that you could proceed to the next station which was Stalbridge.

Pat Holmes

As a passed cleaner in the early 1960s I was rostered to fire to a driver who I was told would sometimes go to sleep on the footplate. On this particular turn we worked a goods train to Blandford Forum ex-Evercreech then changed over approximately at 9.30am with Branksome men, we would then go to Bournemouth West and return with the 11.40am ex-Bournemouth being relieved at Templecombe Junction. We left Broadstone and there I was working away. I looked up and this driver was fast asleep on his seat. I ended up firing and driving through the Dorset countryside a massive BR class 4 4-6-0 No 75027 back to Henstridge, where he finally woke up... some experience when you're only 17 years of age.

STALBRIDGE

Ron Barter

One event in the 1950s that I shall always remember at Stalbridge was just before Christmas. I was a goods porter there and we had a large amount of Christmas mail for the 5pm to Bournemouth. This particular night a fierce gale was blowing. We had all the mail on two four-wheeled barrows. Hubert Tulk, Arthur Sparks the postman and myself were all in the shelter away from the elements, when suddenly we heard a crash. We looked out and saw that one of the barrows had blown onto the track, mail and all. The mail train and another train were almost due. In fact we could see one of the trains approaching. We rushed onto the track and dragged the barrow and mail off, just in time. We didn't have time to put the mail back on the barrow. We just threw bags of mail and parcels going in all directions into the guards van.

Stalbridge signalbox and crossing gates. The platform edge is painted white with some enthusiastic overspill (J F Rimmer)

Eric Miles

I was relief porter at Stalbridge for a while and it was one of my first jobs working on my own initiative. It gave me a chance to try out new skills which I had learnt. One morning the stationmaster informed me that a Lady ****** would be arriving at the station to catch the "Pines Express" and that I had to leave everything else to attend to all her wishes. Well, Lady ****** arrived in her Rolls Royce as the "Pines Express" was approaching. I was rushing around and was loaded down with her cases and hat boxes. After a monumental struggle I found the first class coach and placed her and the luggage into the compartment. I rushed off the train. Her parting words were "my chauffeur has a little something for you, and many thanks for your help". As I got off the train the chauffeur came towards me. In anticipation I moved quickly over to him. He put his hand in his pocket and said "Lady ****** has told me to give you this". I took this grubby rather old three pence piece from his hand. I looked at it as the chauffeur went back to his Rolls Royce. On relating this tale to the porter he said "you were lucky to have got that out of her". Not that I ever looked for tips, as we were paid to give a service. The three pence piece was framed by the station staff with the words "presented to porter Miles by Lady ****** for services rendered".

STURMINSTER NEWTON

Gerald Trowbridge

My days as a junior porter at Sturminster Newton were very interesting. I was 14 years of age when I started in March 1944. My father Frank Trowbridge worked on the S&D for 20 years. He was at Sturminster Newton as a porter then a checker, so the S&D was in my blood at a early age.

I started cleaning out cattle wagons, as a great many cattle came into Sturminster Newton station from Ireland. They were bought by dealers and then fattened up in the water meadows, and later sold for meat. Quite a lot of horses arrived for the market. These mostly travelled in horse boxes on passenger trains. These boxes had a passenger compartment built in which the juniors found was a good place to hide from the senior staff. Two mornings a week, it was my duty to change the lamps for the signals. This meant cleaning the lamps and filling them up with paraffin. There was a lot of walking involved in this job as the distant signals were quite a long way from the station.

During the years 1944 to 1945 the American ambulance trains often ran on the S&D. If I was on lamp duty and one of these trains went through they would throw out through the window to me their K rations, which included gum, chocolate and even cigars.

One of my favourite jobs in the winter, was stoking the fire next to the outside water column which was put there to make sure it wouldn't freeze, which enabled the engines to take water.

I remember there was a horse and dray which delivered the local goods around the town. The driver's name was Jack Francis and the horse's name was "Prince". He was stabled in *The White Hart* public house. A lorry was used to deliver goods to the outlying villages. Bert Witt was the driver. I remember he was partial to chewing twist, which he would then dry and smoke it in his clay pipe. At Sturminster station there was a few characters. One of them was a nice old porter named Walt Fudge. He was 6ft 3ins high. They called him Sticker, because he was long and thin like a stick. When the passenger trains came in, Walt was first in line to get tips from the passengers: he had it worked out to a fine art. I learnt a lot from him.

I remember one incident when I was working in the lamp house, which over the years had become saturated in paraffin. On this particular day I dropped a match and the lamp house was no longer. I had to report it to the stationmaster who was always at a certain time of day to be found taking liquid refreshment at *The White Hart*. I went along to the pub and told him what had happened. He was not amused!

SHILLINGSTONE

Eric Miles

My introduction to the S&D was in 1920s as a young lad, leaving Shillingstone for our annual holiday, being a day at Bournemouth. What a thrill to get our tickets stamped in a ticket machine, then crossing over the line to the down side. Listening to the bells in the signalbox, little did I know that many years later I would be a signalman on the S&D.

Shillingstone signalbox. Note the Whitaker tablet exchange apparatus at the side (J F Rimmer)

I watched the signal being lowered and not forgetting the token (single line) I remember the use of the bells being explained to me by the ever-so-friendly signalman. The train would arrive and we would get aboard: father, mother, younger and older brother and myself. There was no corridor coaches; sometimes a toilet shared between compartments (but not always). Things like that did not worry us as I was too enthralled with the sepia pictures of holiday spots on the walls above the seats. The heater on and off switch and the emergency cord (which pulled unnecessary would cost a sum of £s) and the leather strap for lowering the windows were all part of the exciting journey.

I used to write down the names of the stations as we went by them like Stourpaine Halt which I remember being built. On arrival at Bailey Gate we were always greeted by the call "B. Gate, B Gate" – yes the train trip over the S&D was something that I shall never forget.

Percy Hobbs

The wartime had its darkest moments but everybody carried on with their duties and there was always something to laugh about. I remember the time when a box wagon had a suspected hot box and was put off at Shillingstone down sidings. After a few days the phones began to get hot with people enquiring about a lost box wagon. Eventually this wagon in Shillingstone sidings turned out to be this lost wagon. No wonder everybody was looking for it: it was found to be full of spirits for the officers mess at Blandford army camp and not a drop was missing, because no one knew about it.

Shillingstone 30/8/65 BR class 5 No 73001 waiting to depart with one of the last Bath–Bournemouth holiday specials. This locomotive was fitted with a chime whistle which was a delight to hear. Fireman John Sawyer is looking out of the cab (collection John Sawyer)

George Skinner

There is no way such a railway would be allowed to run today with health and safety concern as it is with the work place, for example. When travelling at speed the exchange of tablets "single line working" at places like Shillingstone on the up side, I always used to hang onto the side handle with one hand, lean out and press down on the catcher with the end of the coal pick handle, with the other hand to prevent the tablet jumping up, as some were inclined to do that when changing the tablet at speed.

Shillingstone: a view of the station building on a summer day in the 1960s with everything neat and tidy, the lawn being mown by a member of staff (J F Rimmer)

Fred Fisher

Stourpaine and Durweston was a halt between Shillingstone and Blandford Forum on the Dorset end of the S&D. The line at that point ran alongside the River Stour which at times overflowed its bank and caused delays on the line. Many times as a driver and fireman I have gone through this halt and stopped there especially for the school children from the local school. A boy from Bryanston school was unfortunately knocked down by a train just outside Stourpaine and had both feet severed. He was lucky to be alive because it took quite a long time to find him after he went missing. I must admit I always kept a sharp look out at the spot where the accident occurred when passing.

Stourpaine was a very bleak place in the winter months and coming to this halt in a loco in pitch darkness was extremely difficult. We used to look out for this light from a nearby farmhouse, which guided us into the halt.

Stourpaine 7/7/62: note the Southern Railway concrete construction (Colin Caddy)

BLANDFORD

Eddie Skinner

Towards 1949 I was at last to have a regular mate: a driver named Alec Bolwell who originally came from Highbridge.

It was a lot better having a regular roster and mate, as you could plan for any occasion that came up. Alec was a very good driver and mate; he was another who would always help you.

I remember an occasion when I was firing to Alec, it was one evening and I remember we were on the last passenger train from Bournemouth West to Templecombe and returned with the last passenger. Our guard was Alfred Metcalf. It was a very bad winter's evening; driving rain and a nasty wind. We had been going up to Blandford, stopping at every station and running well. On leaving Blandford station there was a steady climb out and the line goes in a half circle, right around a farm. On going under the road bridge we felt a bump like we were passing over something. Alec slammed on the brakes and said you had better get down Ted and go back and have a look and see what's up. Down I got – wind, rain, darkness and oil lamp in my hand, I met the guard Alf Metcalf coming up the line, "what's up Ted?" he said. "Alec thinks we have hit something". We made our way down the line; unfortunately we had hit an old gentleman. I believe he was a man of the cloth: on looking up I could see his hat and umbrella neatly placed up against the bridge wall. What a sad way to finish your life.

Arthur Bowen

This particular tale will be remembered as long as there is a S&D man alive. Someone had sent a dog with a label on its collar from Bournemouth to Blandford by passenger train. At Blandford the guard handed the dog with the collar and lead to Joe Penny the porter, who took the dog down the platform into the parcels office. The dog struggled so much that it slipped out of his collar and ran out of the office and down the platform, Joe Penny chasing after him shouting "stop that dog, it's a parcel".

Blandford Forum 6/3/29: derailment of a coal train at Blandford St Mary bridge – the signalbox was not short of coal for a long time after! (collection H Whiting)

An amusing story comes to mind: in the summer of 1951 while I was waiting to take up my job as a signalman at Corfe Mullen, I was working as a relief porter at Blandford. One morning an Indian lady walked into the booking office and asked for a first class ticket to London. Don Ridout the booking clerk handed her the ticket, and said that will be £3 please, the lady put down four £5 notes and she couldn't seem to understand why Don said he did not need all that. £5 notes were then white, £1 notes were green in those days. Don took a £1 note from the till and laid it on the counter beside the £5, and explained to the lady the difference between the two. The lady said that she had been in England for three weeks, and had been using £5 notes for £1 notes ever since she had arrived, and nobody had ever told her the difference.

Tony Axford

We were leaving Blandford near a farm on the high embankment which was above the Shaftsbury Road. My driver Les Cuss and myself were on a Standard class 4 4-6-0 on the up fast from Bournemouth. Looking out of the cab I spotted a rather flustered looking policeman with no helmet on running along on the other side of the fence up above us on the right hand side of the bank. He looked like he was in hot pursuit of somebody. Curious to see if there was anyone running along the other side of the track (we were on a long left hand curve here and I could see what was happening) I strolled over to the other side of the cab and looked over Les's shoulder through the front cab window along the boiler. Sure enough there was a man running as fast as his legs could carry him. He looked like he was trying to outrun the Standard 4 *and* the policeman. Needless to say he was going to come second best. I reached for my shovel and put some coal on it and threw it in the direction of the running man. It hit him fair and square on the body. He immediately crashed head first down the steep embankment through some brambles and that was the last time I saw the poor fellow.

I remember Les told me off and said that I should not have done that, "you could have killed him". I think he was made of rubber because I later read in the Western Gazette that he had jumped out of a first floor window of Blandford police station and they never caught him.

John Stamp

On 10th February 1942 I had the privilege of firing on a Royal train taking King George VI to Blandford to visit the troops stationed there. Being wartime there was great restriction and secrecy and the Royal train was designated by the code name "Grove". I remember being called out in the early morning about 5.30am, as the rostered fireman had failed to report. I got to Bath Green Loco and found the driver was a chap called Walt Lake who was later killed in the Bath blitz in April 1942. The locomotive we had was a Black 5 No 5432. She had been polished up and made to look really smart, I recall clearly that there were three inspectors aboard; one of them drew me to one side and said "Do you know who is on the train?". "No", I replied. He said "It is the King and he is going to Blandford to review his troops. There is to be no smoke and no blowing off, also you are not to divulge about the King's presence to anybody".

We set off about 6.30am; the train consisted of only four cars. All were totally blacked out and completely enclosed. There was guards on every part of the train; two inspectors travelled on the footplate.

We set off from Bath with instructions not to exceed 40mph at any point. All the lines were kept especially cleared for us and I was later informed that a light engine proceeded us at an easy pace to make sure that there was no obstruction or any possibility of a derailment. It was a very dark overcast morning. We arrived at Blandford without any troubles soon after 8.30am in the morning. We pulled the train into Blandford station and the whole platform was covered with people and VIPs awaiting to meet the King on his arrival. I did catch a glimpse of the King leaving the train, he was immediately put into an enclosed car which sped off at high speed. Later we took the train on to Poole where a military guard was placed on the train. Later the loco went to Branksome to turn. We returned back to Poole where it was stabled to await the King. The train was taken over by a Southern crew back to Blandford and there the King was taken to Templecombe, then on to Waterloo via Salisbury. At the end of the day we were congratulated by inspector Arkwright on our performance in the handling of the locomotive.

Norman Rallison

One day when I was relieving at Blandford the Bailey Gate milk train arrived. When the train had left I gave the out of section signal 2.1. No sooner had I done that when the signalman at Shillingstone rang me on the telephone and said "Why have you cleared this train, it has just passed here into my section without a tail lamp on?". I rang the signalbox at Bailey Gate and got hold of the guard of the train and told him. Between ourselves we said it must have fallen off in the section. Next day I walked the line and found the tail lamp, but I found out later they hadn't put one on at Templecombe, so whose lamp it was and how did it come to be there we never found out.

Blandford Forum: 1960s view of the station and signalbox. The station staff seem busy and the goods yard is filled with trucks (JF Rimmer)

Eddie Skinner

I well remember back to the early 1950s there were always photographers taking pictures of us on the footplate. One photographer that stands out in my memory is Ivo Peters; he was always about anywhere between Bath Green Park and Evercreech Junction. Apart from him a group of young boys from the private school at Charlton Marshall had their own camera club at the school.

I was then a regular fireman to driver Alec Bolwell, originally from Highbridge. When we were working slow trains up to Templecombe and back to Bournemouth West, we would arrive at Charlton Marshall Halt and we would often talk with these lads about the photos they had taken. Alec and myself received quite a lot of photos taken by these boys. Unfortunately I lent them to somebody and they were never returned: some of slow trains but most were taken of the fast holiday specials in the summer, one being the "Pines Express". They took most of their pictures over the weekend, especially the Saturday traffic.

There was usually about six boys at Charlton Marshall Halt and with great interest they logged and took photos of all the traffic that was going past the halt at that time.

Charlton Marshall 24/4/65: a general view of the halt looking up the incline (Colin Caddy)

SPETISBURY

Eddie Skinner

A fine driver to work with was Donald Beale. I was frequently booked on to fire for him. He was great from the start, always there to help you whenever he could. Once you was off and running he drove at all times with great care. He never took his eyes off the track.

I remember one trip, it was a "Holiday Special" back from Bath, we had a Stanier Black 5 with 12 coaches on. Well it was Donald's thing that if you had very large lumps of Welsh coal on the tender, you would put them to one side and save them for a platelayer who lived in a cottage at Spetisbury Halt. This was situated down a steep bank along the side of the platform at Spetisbury station. "Right Ted when we get up there at Spetisbury let it go for Charlie." I had the doors open with a lump of Welsh steam coal ready to go, Donald shouted out "let it go!" and I pushed it out with my foot. Down the bank it went gathering speed. Unfortunately it diverted to the right and went straight through Charlie's lovely greenhouse. That was one day that our timing was out! Charlie eventually repaired the greenhouse and there was no hard feelings.

Top: Spetisbury c1957. BR Standard class 5 No 73049 near the halt with the down express. Bottom: Spetisbury 24/4/65. General view of the platforms (Colin Caddy)

George Skinner

I recall an incident which could have ended in a disaster: I was working a down semi-fast from Bath one evening. The driver had a friend at Spetisbury and we used to push off some coal for him. This particular day the driver decided to push this big lump of Yorkshire hard coal off himself. It must have been a half a hundred weight or more. It left the footplate at speed and went down the bank and sailed over the fence. Of course at the time of delivery there was nobody in the garden. However from behind a row of blackcurrant bushes, surprised by the sound of the engines whistle and the first bounce of this lump of coal, appeared the head of the old lady of the house. I saw the face of the driver go white as this huge lump of coal bounced like the bouncing bomb of wartime inventor Barnes Wallis. It went over the old lady's head, bounced once again to disappear through the hedge at the bottom of the garden and the driver by this time was in a state of shock. I well remember thinking of the possible consequences although I can laugh about it now.

BAILEY GATE

Eddie Skinner

One day on early turn we were working the goods to Carter's sidings. I was working with driver Alec Bolwell. We had shunted the milk tanks in place ready to go out into traffic. At Bailey Gate they had a factory for making cheeses. There was always a great many milk tankers arriving in the yard. Having finished all the shunting in the yard, Alec and I were going to have some tea, when the shunter came up onto the engine and said to us that they were having some bother with a bull that was on a wagon on the other side of the yard. He asked us if we would shunt the cattle truck with the bull in to a line nearer the road as some men with a cattle truck were coming to pick it up. When we arrived at the truck, the bull by this time was really going mad. All the old cattle trucks had birch and oak flooring and the uprights were made from Colombian pine. They were very tough, but this bull was kicking it to pieces; its rear legs were smashing up the uprights of the truck. It was some bull; the biggest one I'd ever seen. After the poor old shunter had hitched up this depleted cattle truck, we shunted it over to a line by the road. The lorry had arrived and two old farmers got out and had a look at the bull, who by this time was really going to town; they then backed the lorry near the wagon and proceeded to put up a frail fence between the wagon and the rear of the truck. They just dropped the tail of the lorry down. One of the farmers went up to the side of the wagon and the other one at the rear of the bull. When the chap who was at the side got the ring released from the bull's nose, the other one gave it a whack on the back. Both were shouting like mad. The bull straightened up at the end of the wagon, which was now open. It just ran out of the wagon down the ramp they had laid then it went up onto the other ramp and straight into the lorry. The old Dorset farmer just smacked the tail of the lorry up and said to the bull "Good boy"! It was so easy for them, that I could hardly believe it. The wagon was taken out of service for extensive repairs.

Bailey Gate 24/4/65 BR Standard class 4 No 75073 enters the station with a stopping train (Colin Caddy)

Bailey Gate 1929: the arrival of watercress from Bedford & Jesty in a 1923 Humber van with Harold Whiting on the left (H Whiting collection)

Bill Harford

When I was on a freight train from Bailey Gate to Poole we had gone into Carter's siding which was on the old Wimborne line. Whilst in the sidings I decided to clean the fire. After doing this I filled the firebox with some nice lumps of hard coal and shut the firebox door. After about fifteen minutes I opened it up and had an almighty blow back; it blew back in my face and burnt my eyes. I couldn't see for a few hours. They called an ambulance and I was rushed to Wimborne eye hospital where they had to cut my eyelashes off so I could open my eyes. That accident happened at about 12 o'clock so the railway stopped my wages from then, as they had to send another fireman to continue the journey.

Bailey Gate Crossing 1960s. The signalbox, taken out of service, is looking sad and forlorn – what memories this sight would evoke in signalmen who had worked this box (J F Rimmer)

CORFE MULLEN

Arthur Bowen

I joined the railway in March 1946 at Leeds City LMS. After nationalisation in 1948 Leeds became NE Region so I asked to be transferred back to the Midland but failed. I then applied for the position of relief porter at Blandford Forum on the Somerset and Dorset Railway. In May 1951 I was accepted for the position of relief porter. I covered various country stations: Henstridge, Stalbridge, Sturminster Newton and Bailey Gate. In the October of that year I applied for and obtained the post of signalman at Corfe Mullen.

My time at Corfe Mullen signalbox was full of incidents. One morning when the 9.05am Bristol train was waiting at the down home to cross and the 11.40am Bournemouth West was late, the fireman of the 9.05am came to the signalbox to sign the train register book, Rule 55. After the 11.40 had gone and I had changed the points, I gave the tablet to the fireman and pulled off the home signals. The fireman waited outside the box to get onto the engine, but the train remained at the home signal. Two minutes later it had still not moved, so the fireman walked back up the line to his engine to see what the problem was. When the train went by the fireman indicated to me that the driver had been fast asleep when he had got back to the train.

Corfe Mullen 24/4/65: Ivatt class tank No 41243 on the 12.23 Templecombe–Bournemouth West (Colin Caddy)

Thinking of sleeping reminds me of another incident: it was in the spring of 1952 and I was on early turn 6am to 2pm. I arrived at Corfe box to find the level crossing gates smashed to bits. The permanent way gang were there: 2 signal engineers, 2 telegraph engineers, a signal inspector and the stationmaster from Bailey Gate. It appears that the signalman whom I was due to relieve had accepted the 2.40am freight, Poole to Bath from Broadstone. The running time was 11 to 12 minutes. We used to wait 5 to 6 minutes before opening the crossing gates and pulling off the signals. It appears the signalman sat down in the armchair and must have dozed off. When the train driver approached the distant signal to find it at caution, he applied the brakes to slow down only to find that the brakes had failed. The driver of the train kept his hand on the whistle to warn the guard that something was wrong and also to warn the signalman, but the signalman did not hear the whistle, with the result that the train went through the gates. Everyone was working very hard to clear the line as the "Down Mail" was due at 6.10am. That morning at about 9am the local police constable called at the signalbox to complain about the noise the 2.40am had made. Half the residents of Corfe Mullen had been to his house to complain about the train waking them up.

Funny enough, the same train caused another occurrence; this time I was on nights. The date being September 1952, again the 2.40am Poole freight was coming down the bank the gradient being 1:60, just inside Corfe Mullen's up distant signal. The guard, who had never done this particular turn before, thought the train was travelling too fast, so he applied his brake hard.

The driver when reaching the bottom of the bank seeing he had a clear road, opened the regulator for the up gradient, the resultant snatch caused havoc. It wasn't a coupling that snapped, it was a wagon of coal; the frame broke just above the front axle – and right on the junction points They had to introduce a bus service between Bailey Gate and Broadstone. The line was cleared just before the "Pines Express" was due. The one good thing about the accident was that Corfe Mullen signalbox had plenty of coal all that winter.

Another memory that comes to mind: opposite the side of the crossing gates at Corfe Mullen signalbox was a railway cottage occupied by George Ridout and his wife. George had retired from the S&D in 1930 as a ganger. In 1951 he was 86 years of age, and his wife 88. Every Friday George used to come up to the signalbox with his rent book and one penny: he had a pension from the S&D of 1 shilling a week, his rent was 1s 1d.

Eddie Skinner

One of my most humorous moments was working the Bailey Gate milk train and bringing it back from Carter's sidings, Corfe Mullen. The driver I was with was well known for working at home on his garden, and early mornings was not his best time of day. We were up at Carter's sidings picking up a few trucks of clay. On returning back down the line to Corfe Mullen signalbox, he leaned over the side of his cab and had a big yawn. In doing so his false teeth fell out onto the track. On reaching Corfe Mullen signalbox run by Fox Andrew, he told Fox what had happened and of course we were falling about laughing. Fox said he would get the ganger to go down the track and have a look for them. So off we went to finish our shift. Three days later the driver and myself were on duty for the same shift. Jock the steamraiser came into the cabin and said to him "there's a parcel here for you". Sure enough: a small cardboard box about four inches square with a big railway label on it addressed to him. He opened the box and there were his false teeth, all wrapped up neatly in cotton wool. Smiling broadly, as only he could, he put his teeth into his mouth and off we went again. Needless to say it was a long time before he lived that down.

Fred Fisher

A memory that comes to mind was when we knocked down Corfe Mullen crossing gates. It was in the 1950s, I was firing to driver Lou Long, we were on a

7F with 50 coal wagons on behind us; it was a heavy load to carry. On approaching Corfe Mullen signalbox she started to run away. We went through the distant and the home signal which were both on. We furiously sounded the whistle to attract the attention of the signalman to no avail. Of course we were still trying to bring the train to a standstill at this time. Unfortunately the 7F smashed through the crossing gates which disappeared under the wheels and shattered into small pieces. We finally brought the train under control, I got off the footplate and went back to the box to have a word with the signalman who had come out of his signalbox and was now looking at the damage. A few weeks later on one of our rest days Lou and myself had to attend an inquiry into the incident. We were cleared of any blame. I cannot recall the outcome of this incident.

1957: BR Standard class 4 No 75072 leaving Corfe Mullen – the fireman's efforts must be a little exuberant as the loco is blowing off (Colin Caddy)

CREEKMOOR HALT

Fred Fisher

We used to work the night train from Poole to Templecombe Junction: this was made up of about fifty empty coal wagons. There was a chap who worked for Sykes pottery; he operated a kiln there. This pottery company was adjacent to Creekmoor Halt station and we got to know him when stopping there with passenger trains in the daytime. When working this night turn he would make up a bottle of tea for us. When pulling this heavy train you could only manage walking pace as you went through the station, which enabled him to pass up the bottle of tea for us. It was certainly needed and kept us going for the rest of the journey. It was a nice gesture I thought.

BRANKSOME

Eddie Skinner

After I came out of the forces I went looking for work. I saw the manager of my local labour exchange at Poole and after much debate he said "Mr Skinner, we have a nice job down the coal mines in South Wales for you, or we have a vacancy for a cleaner on the Somerset and Dorset Railway at Branksome loco". Needless to say I replied "I'll take the railway job". In March 1947 I started work at Branksome as a cleaner, I immediately built up a rapport with the older railwaymen there; they were all very helpful.

My first memory was with driver Arthur Clist. At 4am in the morning I'd fallen asleep in the cabin and driver Clist was not amused. He was well known for making sure that his engine was well prepared, and couldn't understand other people who were not up to his high standards. He was right of course. I must say I learnt a lot from Arthur; he was a gentleman to work with and when you fired to him, he would help you throughout the journey whatever turn you were on. He was well noted from Bath to Bournemouth as a very conscientious driver. Sometimes the chaps at the other end at Bath would bring the engine into Bournemouth not oiled. Arthur, being what he was, would oil up the engine when it arrived.

Arthur was a man that never swore, but all he used to say to me was "Edward, Edward, this shocking engine has no shocking oil in there again, them shocking Bath men". He was a great man and well remembered.

Branksome 4/7/59: Black 5 No 44937 stands ready to leave the shed with driver Archie Gunning and fireman Brian Smith (collection Archie Gunning)

Percy Hobbs

I remember one trip in 1941: I was firing to driver Len Counsell and our locomotive power was a 7F. We were on the night goods to Poole and had pulled off at Branksome Junction. We had gone light engine from Poole round to Bournemouth Gas Works. We had Midland lamps on this engine. The procedure was that we had to take the red shade out of the lamp on the back of the engine and put it on the lamp on the front of the engine before the signalman would allow the dummy to be pulled off to enable you to come back round to go to Bournemouth West Junction.

This particular night the Germans were very busy overhead. They were bombing all the way to Southampton. I was making my way to the front of the engine to change the shade on the lamp. I heard the whistling of a Jerry bomb coming my way, ducked and hit my head against the 7Fs coupling, cutting my forehead badly.

Fortunately the bomb exploded nearby. I picked myself up and crawled back onto the footplate. My driver Len Counsell was sitting on his seat arms folded with a big grin on his face. He looked at me and said "Percy it is a pity the resources of the world couldn't be used for a better purpose". I never forgot that.

PYLLE

Bill May

Pylle was a small station with two platforms; the down one had a shelter for the passengers; the other had a brick and stone building containing the station, booking office and waiting room, and at the end of the station there was a signalbox. The goods yard had two sidings and a goods shed; at the end of the goods shed the stationmaster's house was built. The traffic was coal and green timber trunks from the local estate. Hunting was done in this section and when it was taking place a notice was placed on the notice board at our signing-on office in Highbridge. The notice indicated to us to keep a sharp lookout for hounds on the track. It has been said that if a train had to stop because of the hounds the driver was given 10 shillings by the huntsman.

I remember working an Allotment Members Excursion on one of my favourite engines: a class 3F Bulldog No 48. We were going from Bridgwater to Portsmouth and had 12 coaches on. She was a good engine; I remember she took them over Pylle bank and never took a bit of notice of it.

Pylle 1960s: a general view of the station from under the roadbridge carrying the A37. The crossing loop and sidings have been removed. Unfortunately these substantial buildings were never used to their full potential but they still stand as relics of a past age (J F Rimmer)

I recall another incident when I was working a Class 4 Armstrong in the bad winter of 1963. We were on the 6.15pm Evercreech to Highbridge running into Pylle. At the railway bridge there was a drop both sides of the line causing a culvert and the wind blew the snow off the fields into it. I felt I was running into something but just managed to get through. I heard later that the last passenger train to Evercreech station from Pylle ran into it and couldn't go no further.

Referring to Pylle station, it was the first to become redundant. The section was then extended to Evercreech Junction. Later Pylle turned into a halt and one porter was left in charge working a split turn, early and late. The stationmaster's house became vacant allowing the porter to live there. This is how it remained until the line closed.

WEST PENNARD

West Pennard 1953: Paul Fry, clerk, and stationmaster Reg Jeans pose at the back of the station building in front of a 1933 Morris Minor
(collection P Fry)

Paul Fry

I remember well my time at West Pennard, having been transferred there from Wells Priory Road about 1950, after having done a very short apprenticeship under Cyril Jenkins and the chief clerk George Parker. George used to live in Wincanton and caught the train up to Masbury every morning and cycled down to Wells from there.

Having learned what I could of the trade in the booking office and in the goods department, I was summoned one day to see Charles Wellington Broome the GWR stationmaster who had responsibility for Wells Tucker Street and also Priory Road. I was duly informed that from the next Monday I would be working at West Pennard under the well known stationmaster Reg Jeans. They gave me a one way free pass from Wells to West Pennard via Glastonbury. I must admit that I was a bit taken aback at the news, as I had not expected to have to uproot myself from the cosy existence at Wells, living in the old S&D station house just 20 yards from work. Anyhow, I obtained myself a bicycle and my father guard Glencoe William Charles Fry (always called "Bob") had a chat with Reg Jeans so the path was made smooth. I duly presented myself at West Pennard station on a Monday morning at 9am in the booking stationmaster's office. I was made welcome and given simply tasks to do, the first of which was to enter up the delivery sheets for the goods that had arrived and were waiting to go out on the lorry driven by Jim Lindsey.

Jim was quite a character: he created enormous amounts of humour as sometime later he had all his teeth taken out and a top and bottom set fitted. He called them his tombstones and never really got used to them. Most of the staff at West Pennard liked a drop of the local scrumpy except me, who having had one mouthful could not stand the taste and still cannot to this day.

One of the big cider producers was W T Allen who always brought their barrels down to the station in their own lorry. In the cab of the lorry was the jar from which the porters helped themselves. I soon learnt that there was a strict pecking order in which the jar could be had. Those that did the unloading and had most contact with the firm went first, then some was put aside for the porter on the different shift and if the boss (stationmaster) wanted some he was served. The jar was then available to others till it was empty. A row broke out one day when the late porter discovered that his opposite number had taken the lion's share and had topped up his share with water.

I do recall the time when a relief lorry driver drove rather swiftly into the station approach and a large barrel of cider came off and rolled at some speed down the road and into the station building. The barrel broke open and all the cider was lost. Tears were shed by the porters at the waste of good cider!

Reg Jeans, the stationmaster, was a very well known S&D character with a great history, super to work with, quite easy going and very sociable.

Top: West Pennard 1963 with Ivatt tank No 41296 entering the station with the Highbridge–Evercreech Junction train. Bottom: ex-GWR pannier tank with the Evercreech Junction–Highbridge train. Within a short time the passing loop and sidings would be removed (Colin Caddy)

One thing you had to look out for was the security of the cash in the office. Reg used to like to creep back from one of his walks to the signalbox or goods shed and quietly slip into the office to see if the till had been left unattended. Once I left the till unattended only to find on my return that all the money had gone. It was only handed back after a stern lecture on the safety of property: a lesson I always, even to this day, remember.

Reg was also a cartoonist of some fame and used to do sporting caricatures of local FA divisional teams for the "Green un" and the "Pink un" (the Bristol evening papers). I also seem to remember that he did the local skittle teams on the wall of the skittle alley at *The Railway Hotel* (now called *The Apple Tree*) at West Pennard.

The only near disaster that I recall at the station was when the mid morning goods train from Evercreech Junction, which conveyed the road-box from station to station, had just arrived. The guard left his brake-van to have a chat with Reg on the platform; the porter/shunter cut off the wagons next to the engine for shunting into the yard. The train engine pulled forward, and was just coming back and across into the shed road, when I noticed that the portion of the train still in the station had started to roll down the gradient on the very straight line towards Glastonbury. The guard had not screwed down the guard's van brake hard enough and they were off.

I shouted from the booking office doorway to Reg and the guard, and with commendable speed and agility Reg was off down the line pinning down brakes as hard as he could, leaping goat wise over the obstructions as he went, the guard leaping for all his worth onto the van to try and get some more purchase on the van-brake. The whole outfit was stopped about 10 yards from the catch points at the end of the loop. It was discovered later that the van brake was faulty. Reg was quite blasé about the whole event, saying that, as he had been a shunter for some time at Water Orton marshalling yard on the Midland, the ability to run at full speed over the track came back to him quickly.

I left Pennard and was transferred back to Wells Priory Road to the goods office having had my education extended in many ways. My days at West Pennard were mostly idyllic, not too rushed; if we had a few passengers we were delighted! We all got on very well with each other and the regular tradesmen using the station yard. I do wish that I had been more aware of what was happening all around me and had taken more notice of everything, but in younger days everything seemed so permanent and we thought it would last for ever, never dreaming that it would almost all be swept away in time. If I could turn the clock back for a spell of weeks I would go back to West Pennard willingly.

Maurice Cook

A light-hearted moment that I can remember was a trip to Evercreech on the 10am; we rode on the cushions where we were to relieve two Templecombe men. As it was in wartime we had some Southern tank engines for this duty. To put the blower on these locos you had to turn it two or three times before it worked. We thought something was funny as we were running into West Pennard station too fast. I looked out of the carriage window and saw flames coming out both sides of the cab. Anyway we did stop at West Pennard. Tom Kesteven was the fireman on this particular train and he had managed to get hold of the pricker and pull the fire doors shut to stop the flames coming out. The blower had not come on and it had caused a blow back. When we arrived at Evercreech we went to investigate to see what the problem was. There was Tom saying to himself "Look at my coat, look at my coat!" His black coat had been hanging up in the cab and there was now only about 3 inches of his coat left including the hanger. The blackout curtains were burnt to bits and the whole cab was black with soot, but it was so funny: old Tom kept saying "Look at my coat, look at my coat!"

Fred Lester

In the 1940s the LMS was the ruling body over the S&D. Their headquarters were at Derby, and I wrote to them asking for a job. After some months waiting for a local vacancy, I joined the S&D on the 8th January 1940. I was offered a job as a junior clerk at West Pennard station. The rate of pay was £55 per annum, and I gladly accepted the position: I had started my S&D career which was to last for 25 years.

Also in the area were two large cider makers and I frequently saw the platform filled with barrels, awaiting loading. The return of empties was a constant source of trouble, as many showed no point of origin.

Local deliveries of goods arriving for the station were performed by horse-drawn flat drays and when a particular horse and driver had been together for many years the horse was as familiar with the routine as the driver. It would go from shop to shop stopping without command at all the regular places. One very popular round was the weekly delivery of barrels of beer to all the pubs, and there were a lot more of these in the days gone by. It was the practice of the publican to reward the man with a drink after the barrels had been safely loaded into the cellars. One can imagine the effect after about 10 such calls. They used to tell the story of one elderly carter named Wallace, whose horse and dray returned to the station yard and pulled up in its usual place; there was no sign of the driver, he had fallen asleep in a cellar after too much ale!

His horse had waited the usual amount of time and then had set off in the familiar way back down the road to the station. Wallace is said to have woken up and stumbled outside and exclaimed "some bugger has stole me 'orse!"

As in many work places a new lad had to be initiated, so in my first week I was offered a large three-handled cider cup, with everybody urging me "go on lad, drink it all down. It'll do thee good". Never again! That cycle ride home to Glastonbury was one that I will never forget.

Lighting on country stations was by oil lamps, and in the office we had a Tilley lamp, which was pumped up to make pressure vapour. The incandescent gas type mantle gave a reasonably white light and after you got it started it was hung on a hook from the ceiling. I shared a small office at West Pennard with the stationmaster, Robert Hayes. One evening when the lamp had been in use for a while, I looked up to see the stationmaster standing on his chair searching for something on the top shelf which was almost at ceiling level, when suddenly he fell to the floor, I helped him up and took him outside for some fresh air. Apparently what had happened was that the lamp had not been working efficiently and caused a build up of vapour at ceiling level.

Early in the war, we formed a Railway Home Guard Platoon. At first we had no rifles, but full of enthusiasm and vigour we mounted guards on bridges carrying shunting poles.One of our First World War veterans was a man called Guy Parsons. He became a sergeant when we received rifles and ammunition and he undertook training at Glastonbury. One memorable Sunday morning a group of us were gathered together in the stationmaster's office for instruction on parts of the rifle. Sergeant Parsons showed us how the bolt closed locking a bullet in the breech, but it was not a blank, and luckily for us it was pointed up at the ceiling! Being in a confined space the noise was deafening. Afterwards it was often necessary to show that little hole in the ceiling to those who refused to believe the story.

Also at West Pennard there had been the odd fully-booked excursion train that ran non-stop from Evercreech to Highbridge, but the branch was not prepared for the appearance of the first of the "Barbed Wire Specials" in the 1940s: 30 or more open wagons piled high with coils of barbed wire, rattling through at speeds that no freight trains had done before. The signalman had to enlist the help of a porter to stand at the far end of the platform to accept the token while he handed out the new one at his end. The station certainly came alive when these specials came through at high speed. Coastal defences had become a priority and this barbed wire was destined for the south west.

I remember an enemy aircraft returning from a raid, and releasing a bomb which landed about half a mile away on Pennard Hill. Fortunately it was away from the village and the track. All this was part of the early war years at West Pennard station.

GLASTONBURY

LMS class 3F 0-6-0 No 43194 ready to leave Glastonbury Station in 1958 with two coaches. The four platform trolleys transported the boxes of Clarks shoes from their nearby factory (Colin Caddy)

Fred Lester

The last months leading up to closure of the S&D were a bad time at Glastonbury station. I had worked on the S&D for 25 years as a goods and booking clerk. There was to be no more freight trains rumbling into the station with timber from Avonmouth Docks for delivery to John Snow & Co, timber merchants. The friendship of the station staff would be sorely missed, workmates like signalmen Eric Miles and Harry Jeans whose son Reg was the stationmaster at Evercreech New. It was natural we should resent any move by management to close "our line". It wasn't just a job; it was a way of life, especially for my family.

My father was a porter at Wells Priory Road in the 1920s, later to become a guard. I recall enjoying unofficial rides with him on the push and pull service between Wells and Glastonbury. In those days Glastonbury station boasted a newspaper kiosk and on the island platform between the Evercreech and Wells line there was a refreshment room.

When I was younger I used to enjoy going with my father to his allotment which was next to the goods yard at Glastonbury. Most of the S&D railwaymen had a plot there. While my father was enjoying his gardening I would go to the far end of the allotment and watch the trains go by.

The station staff of Glastonbury in latter years consisted of two signalmen, one for each shift; similarly you had two foremen, two porters, office staff, crossing keeper and (the stationmaster) Mr Killeby. Wages were not high but it adds up to a considerable expenditure just for one country branch station.

There are still a few bits of the track route easily recognizable together with two bridges, but most unique perhaps is the restored canopy from the central platform re-erected in Glastonbury's central market area.

LMS class 3F 0-6-0 No 43436 with a passenger train, August 1958. Note the Tor on the left (Colin Caddy)

ASHCOTT

Sam Lane

One of my uncles who lived at Wells and worked on the S&D in the early 1900s told me how on a Sunday if they were working at Ashcott they would have to walk it; 10 miles there and 10 miles back. There was no transport in them days, they didn't know any different; they would cut across fields, they knew all the short cuts – hard times in them days.

SHAPWICK

Norah Cook

When the war had finished, Vic Newman my predecessor, whose job as a booking clerk I had taken over, returned and I was sent down the line to Shapwick. That was in 1946. There was not many passengers but there was large consignments of peat to be billed; it kept me busy. The booking office was large and the only light was from an oil lamp, but it was quite comfortable and there was a roaring fire to keep you warm. The stationmaster was a Mr Beake and the porter was Aubrey Simmons. I remember in 1948, it was a bad winter, and on one occasion I caught the usual 10am train to Shapwick, but the snow was getting deeper and deeper, so I am afraid I caught the next train back to Highbridge. I did not fancy spending the night in the station.

Shapwick August 1958: 0-6-0 3F No 43436 with the Highbridge train waiting for the Evercreech train to arrive (Colin Caddy)

Eric Miles

I was a signalman at Shapwick on the S&D branch line. The station and signalbox gave one an image of brightness as they were situated in open countryside. The buildings were made of timber and painted off-white. There was a level crossing worked from the box by a wheel (like many other boxes), the area was very level and one had a good view of the up and down lines. There was a crossing loop, a small goods yard, and a siding, the main goods traffic being agriculture and peat. At the back of the box on the right hand side facing Highbridge was the old canal: it was a haven for wild life, swans, moorhens and lots of water-based animals; in season the mayflies were a problem when they came into the signalbox. We had drinking water at the station and signalbox but no electric power so we had to make use of Tilley lamps which was the signalman's job to trim, fill and light; two for the box and two for each platform.

There was a porter during the day who trimmed the signal lamps and issued tickets. Unfortunately there were not many to issue. The signalman was responsible for unlocking the station waiting room and locking up at night. The box opened at 6am and closed around 10pm which meant there were two shifts.

Norman Rallison

The first time I had a duty at Shapwick I accepted the 11.40am goods from Glastonbury, and got the road ahead signals off. When the goods train arrived and stopped outside the box, I said to the driver "Have you got some wagons to come off?" he said "No, we always stop here and have our dinner", so I put them into the sidings and off they went to the pub across the road for an hour.

Shapwick 29/8/64: full marks to the permanent way gang (Colin Caddy)

EDINGTON JUNCTION

Maurice Cook

One wartime recollection that sticks in my mind, I was with my mate Lou Moxey we were working what we called the "Market Train" from Highbridge. We were travelling along and Lou said to me "What's this over here?" so I went over his side of the footplate and looked out and there were big clouds of dust going up in the air at Edington Junction. I said "that's bombs".

We went on a bit further towards Huntspill crossing where they stopped us and said "some bombs have dropped up there so go careful in case the line has been blocked". So we went on a bit further. We saw a German aircraft being shot down by one of our planes. The British plane came very near to us and carried

Edington Junction pre-1952 as it used to be with signalbox and signals when the Bridgwater branch was extant
(collection Will Locke)

out a victory roll. We later learnt the German plane had come down at Huntspill; anyway we got as far as Edington with this goods train. The signal was at danger so I walked towards the signalbox and on my way in I was picking up pieces of shrapnel that was still very hot. I went into the signalbox, which was manned by Tom Mogg – he was very frightened. He had been in his little shelter when the bomb went off damaging his signalbox instruments. Nearby was a gate that was smashed to bits, further up the line towards Shapwick at Catcott Crossing a bomb had dropped there and blew up the track. My father was stopped at the next station at Shapwick.

It was some time before they restored the line to working order. I suggested they took some of the rail off the sidings at Edington which they did to replace the ones that were broken. Tom Mogg was very lucky that day.

Edington Burtle 21/8/63: very young trainspotters look on at Ivatt tank No 41296 standing with the Evercreech Junction train. Note by this time the loop had been removed (Colin Caddy)

At Highbridge Loco a raffle was held each week to help fund anyone who was off sick. One afternoon when I arrived to work the late passenger train, I was told I had won a chicken from the draw. Apart from the fact that the bird wasn't breathing it was in its natural state. I knew it was no good taking it home like that but fortunately my mate that day was Johnnie Rice. He said he would pluck it for me and he did this whilst we were going from Highbridge to Edington Junction where his mother at that time was the crossing keeper. Johnnie passed the bird out to her asking if she would finish the job and on our return journey from Evercreech Junction Mrs Rice passed the plucked and drawn bird back to us. As it was near Christmas this was my lucky day.

Edington Burtle: general view of the station looking towards Highbridge. A very pretty building in such a remote area. The one remaining siding can be seen in the background (Colin Caddy)

BASON BRIDGE

Mike Baker

Working on the Highbridge branch was always enjoyable. I regarded it as a nice rest from working on the main line. After leaving Evercreech Junction there was a slight gradient up to Pylle, and then the line went down Pylle Bank to West Pennard. From there to Highbridge the line was virtually level and firing was a very leisurely business, although a good head of steam was required to negotiate Pylle Bank on the return journey. The Ivatt 2-6-2 tanks used on the branch almost exclusively in the early 1960s were always in good order right up to the end. Their riding quality was so good; I think we were just as comfortable on the footplate as the passengers were in the coaches.

Bason Bridge Station with the milk factory on the left in August 1964 (Colin Caddy)

One Saturday afternoon Pat Evans and myself had worked out to Highbridge, then back to Bason Bridge to collect milk tanks. We placed the tanks in the GWR yard at Highbridge and were returning light engine to Templecombe. The weather was beautiful and we were both enjoying a quiet ride through the countryside. In the distance I noticed the gates of one of the level crossings was against us. I then noticed the signal protecting the crossing was in the "off" or "all clear" position. I pointed this out to Pat who viewed the situation with disbelief, "don't touch the whistle" he said, as he shut off steam. We approached the crossing very quietly expecting the crossing keeper to appear and open the gates before we got there but there was no sign of life.

Pat stopped the loco about three feet from the crossing gates, climbed down from the footplate and walked to the crossing keeper's cottage and knocked on the door. After a short pause the crossing keeper came to the door. Pat enquired if he needed any firewood. The crossing keepers eyes lit up. "Have you got some?" he said. "No, but you bloody soon will have if you pull off your signal without opening the gates" exploded Pat, pointing to our engine whose presence had seemed to have escaped the crossing keeper's attention. The crossing keeper then explained that the levers were on the other side of the track from the cottage and it was a bit of a nuisance having to go over to pull them as he knew what time the trains ran. He then said "What were we doing with a light engine on the branch at this time on a Saturday afternoon anyway?"

The gates were eventually opened and we were on our way again. I don't think Pat reported the incident. We talked about it afterwards and decided it was too unbelievable, perhaps we were dreaming as we rolled across the peat moors that sunny Saturday afternoon, but it really did happen.

HIGHBRIDGE

Maurice Cook

Highbridge: fireman Keith Conibeer and driver Maurice Cook pose happily on the footplate of LMS class 3F 0-6-0 No 43194 (collection M Cook)

The Yanks were at Highbridge loco and when I was on nights one of the Americans used to come into the messroom. One night he came in (we used to call him "Smoky" because he was always black with grease) and he was extra dirty this particular evening. I said to him "What have you been doing tonight then, Smoky?" and he said "They've been pulling me through those god-damned tubes again." We all laughed. The Americans had a PX store at the loco and it was quite handy for us that smoked; we used to pay 12s 6d for 200 American cigarettes.

My father Ernest Cook was a driver on the S&D at Highbridge and I wanted to follow in his footsteps. He told me there was a vacancy at Highbridge for a bar boy and a caller up. I was 14 and due to leave school in the August holidays. The loco foreman Harry Moorman came to the school and asked my teacher if I could finish a fortnight early which was arranged.

Highbridge 29/8/64: a general view looking back to the Western station end – even Hawksworth coaches were now appearing on the S&D (Colin Caddy)

I started at the loco on Friday the 13th July 1934 at 10pm; I was on nights; your dinner break was between 2am to 3am and you finished at 7am. My first night on was very strange – the different smell of the flare and gas lamps and hot engines. I worked with the steamraiser cleaning fireboxes and shovelling ashes off the brick arches. Each night I was supplied with a small can of rape oil to burn in my flare lamp as this was not as smoky as paraffin. I also had to replace any fire bars that had become burnt or twisted. I had to start calling up the footplate men from their homes from 3.30am onwards. I was supplied with a bicycle for this job and as it only had paraffin burning lamps for lights there was a problem when it was windy; they would blow out leaving you to ride around in the dark. My wages at that time was 16/10d.

Other lads who started at the same time as me were A Williams who was at Bath, Ray Stokes at Templecombe and Maurice Mogg who was a junior porter at Burnham-on-Sea station.

At 6.25am the engine for the first passenger left the loco. I used to deliver the letters to the guard in the guards van of this train. If I was lucky I would get a ride on the footplate or even allowed to drive it. When I returned back to the loco shed I used to clean a firebox of a class 3, which had been disposed about 11pm. I left this one for my last job as sometimes it would have 30 to 40 lbs worth of steam and would still be quite hot. When cycling home after getting that hot the air would feel like ice.

One morning I was cycling home when the basket I carried with my sandwiches and bottle of tea jammed between my knee and the handlebars; I went flying through a fence and onto an allotment. I was careful after that.

Highbridge Works had been closed for a number of years but a lot of things were still in evidence, like a stationary engine with a fly wheel 15ft in diameter and 1ft wide. It was still shiny, this was used to supply power for the gantry in the erecting shop and other machines. It was a sad sight.

A lot of trouble was caused to the water supply to Highbridge loco. It was taken from the River Brue. The lock gates at the Clyce worked with the tide and when too much salt water got into the river it caused the steam engines to prime: a white salt deposit oozed from the plugs and joints. To overcome this a water train was organized. This consisted of four tenders which was taken to Wells to be filled. The drain in the pit under the sheer legs was cemented over and the steamraiser would undo a plug under a tender and fill up the pit. We then had a Petter oil engine which pumped the water through a pipe over the top of the stores into the water tank. After some time water was taken from the town's supply and a booster pump was fitted under the tank; this was a big help when boilers were being washed out. At the back of the loco there was a reservoir which could be an emergency supply of water. It was also used for fire fighting practice; a pump house nearby would pump water from the River Brue to the water tank reservoir for fire fighting. The reservoir contained quite a lot of fish and ducks; there was roach, carp, moorhens and coots.

One of the three steamraisers I worked with used to put wires down to catch rabbits behind the loco shed. He also put dead lines in the river to catch eels. Lots of birds used to nest in a small wooden building and if you walked down to the reservoir in the early morning they would swoop down on you as if to say keep out, this is our domain.

One Sunday night I had a nasty experience, I was cleaning the tube plates on a Templecombe engine, class 3 No 3228 when I noticed smoke coming past me. I then saw the sack that I always put on the fire hole ring in flames. With my chipping hammer I raked it in and got out of the firebox as quickly as possible. My flare lamp must have touched it when I was getting in feet first. When I found the steamraiser and told him, he said "Oh, I can light her up then".

After a while when in a firebox I could tell what coal had been used. Somerset coal (mostly Radstock) would cling as hard ash to the tube plates and crown stays; it would be like a brown colour. Welsh coal kept the boxes much cleaner and would leave a grey white colour. Tredegar and Bedwas coal was a very good quality. One of the steamraisers, a former miner, when tapping a truck of these coals would chalk it on the side of the truck for all to see. North country coal would leave an almost red deposit and the ash on the brick arch would be as fine as sand.

In the running shed a sand furnace always kept burning and a long handled shovel was used to take fire from the furnace and carried on one's shoulder to pass up to the waiting steamraiser. A supply of limestone was always kept near the water tank, a bucket or two to be thrown into the firebox by the fireman when Somerset coal was being used. This was done to prevent clinker sticking to the fire bars. Some nights when a lot of rain had fallen the gas lights would go very dim or go out completely. We then had to lift up a heavy steel cover and, with a long handled box spanner, open the tap to let the water run from the gas mains. This sometimes would be running for a couple of hours with us checking whilst re-lighting the gas lamps. I was recently asked what the white circle on an old photo on the top outside wall of Highbridge running shed was for; this was to reflect light from the gas lamps. A fixed metal ladder was used to reach the lamp and on a wet or windy night trying to re-light the lamps was no joke.

One driver that I recall had just oiled the shaft of class 3 No 3218 and had just come out of the pit when the bottom front mudhole joint blew out with a mighty roar of steam and water. A minute of so before and the driver's back would have been inches away from this joint.

My first job as a call boy started at 3.30am in the morning. You started this time as the first job of the day was the 5.30am goods. The driver who did this turn more than anybody else kept a farm and was always milking his cows when I called on him. In the winter time the narrow road leading to his farm was very dark and one morning three large cart horses were standing in the middle of the road looking at me rather menacingly. As they were much bigger than me I made a long detour to call the driver. It was also on this road one early morning that I had a nasty shock; I was making my way down the road when there was a loud squawk from a goose that I had not noticed; it really gave me the fright of my life.

One particular driver was very hard to wake up; he could not hear the knock, so I used a piece of stone to knock on the wall, then I could hear his wife calling him and he would shout "OK, OK I can hear you!"

His mate was always up doing exercises and would ask me in for a cup of tea. To pass the time between calls on fine mornings I would cycle back to the loco, but if it was pouring with rain I would wait in a shop doorway.

Some drivers and firemen lived outside the calling area and I had to check that they had checked in; if they hadn't we had to call on someone else to do their turn. In the summer months some men came from Bescot, Saltley and Barrow Road sheds. They would be on loan for firing duties. If they were not in lodgings they would sleep in coaches and used to ask me to give them a call, but usually before that time they would get cold and come into the messroom for a warm. At that time there were six large trestle type tables left in the messroom. When the works was open a large fire at each end kept it warm, the fender at our end being a tyre of an engine cut in half. One of the steamraisers used to pick leaves from a plant called coltsfoot then place them on the fender to dry, then put some in his pipe to smoke. Friday nights the tables would be scrubbed and this was a good chance to scrub our overalls on them.

After about five years of nights I had two days as a cleaner and then was made a passed cleaner, which allowed me to do firing turns, and later I was made a fireman.

In May 1943 at the age of 23 I was passed by inspector Arkwright to drive passenger and goods trains. The test for this was to answer questions on rules and regulations and name all the parts of an engine that the inspector pointed to. In theory you had to take down one side of an engine's motion in an emergency which meant you had to make it work on one side only. The inspector would ask you to make various types of trimmings for use in big ends, eccentrics and side rods. You were asked to replace a water and site feed glass. On the next day you had to drive a passenger and goods train to prove to the inspector that you could do the job to his satisfaction.

On each promotion you had to travel to Bath to be examined by the company doctor. I remember on one occasion when the doctor had asked me to drop my trousers, the receptionist started to open the doors and I hastily pulled up my trousers. My father said "They were testing your hearing".

Highbridge 9/1/65: a train has arrived on a wet day hauled by Collett 0-6-0 loco – a sister loco to the left awaits departure to Evercreech Junction (Colin Caddy)

Norah Cook

I joined the S&D in wartime. I was a passenger clerk at Highbridge station in 1942. The job entailed issuing tickets, and sending parcels out. These were mostly from a bacon factory in Highbridge to various NAAFI's in the south and north of England.

I used to make up pay bills on Mondays, for wages and salaried staff. I also helped the stationmaster count the wages and put them into the employees' numbered tins. They then came to the booking office window to collect their wages and drop their empty tins into a tea chest provided for this purpose.

I also paid out the wages to the locomotive staff; there must have been a couple of dozen of them, one of whom was my husband, there was also two signal and telegraph persons, Tom Strike and Tom Bass. Despite the fact that it was wartime I always had a huge coal fire in my office. During the winter months the footplate crews were very generous with the coal. The waiting room on the down platform was quite large and usually a good fire was in there too, courtesy of foreman Mark Hawkins and Walt Lee.

My father Joseph Lush was also on the S&D, he was stationmaster at Burnham-on-Sea and Highbridge, and also harbourmaster at Highbridge Wharf. He was a very tall man with white hair. They used to call him snow white and the seven dwarfs, as quite a few of the staff were much shorter than him. He was also a captain in the Highbridge Home Guard Platoon; we even had a telephone installed at home in case he was needed.

I remember on one occasion he got called out, there was fear that the Germans had invaded, but of course that was a false alarm. Some of the other members of the platoon were Ernest Cook (who was my father in law), Maurice Cook (who later became my husband), driver George Wheadon and booking clerk Victor Newman, my predecessor.

One day the war came a bit too close to Highbridge station: there was a search light battery at Highbridge, and a German plane machine-gunned down the beam. When I got to the station the next morning for work, I noticed there were bits chipped out of the stone footbridge, which went from the S&D side to the Great Western. One of the carriage doors was also smashed. At that time there was loads of American troops around. They more or less took over the loco. They had sidings there where I think they kept all the stores and ammunition. I often wondered if that was what the Germans were after that particular evening.

Highbridge 26/8/64: a train of milk tanks being transferred from the Western region yard on to the S&D for Bason Bridge. This loco is No 2218 (Colin Caddy)

One train I remember coming into Highbridge was from Paddington. Its arrival time was 3.10pm. It was supposed to connect with our 4.00pm passenger train to Evercreech Junction, however it was not unusual for the Paddington train to be late. The railway staff tried to hang on for the 4 o'clock train for as long as they could, and then reluctantly let it go. The passengers then had to wait until 6.50pm for the next train. When this happened we tried to be as helpful as possible to them, in the winter months we took them into the waiting room and made sure the fire was well stoked up.

Shortly after this a vacancy occurred at Highbridge goods office, and I was transferred there, which was much more convenient as by this time I had married driver Maurice Cook, and the goods office was right near our home. The chief clerk was Arthur Jackson, who used to travel from Weston-Super-Mare each day, and the other clerk was Ron King.

A special occasion comes to mind, it was on the 28th August 1954. It was the centenary of the opening of the line between Glastonbury and Highbridge, Clark's the shoemakers organised a special train to run from Glastonbury to Burnham-on-Sea. Members of the Clark family dressed up in period costumes, the engine crew were driver Bill Peck and my husband Maurice Cook, who both wore large beards. I was on the platform at Burnham-on-Sea with our son; all the local dignitaries were there, it was a real family affair, a day to remember.

Most of the goods trains consisted of cattle cake, which lorry drivers Alf Gannicott and Arthur Napper distributed to the many farms in the area. Of course there was also consignments of coal and timber from Highbridge Wharf.

Unfortunately for me the cattle cake was my undoing; I developed asthma and my doctor thought that the cattle cake dust was probably the cause, so I left the S&D. I had so enjoyed my short time on this lovely railway.

Sam Lane

It seems a long time ago now when I first started at Highbridge Works on the 24th May 1924 just a lad of 14 starting my apprenticeship. My first job at the works was in the sawmill making firelighters. There was three of us. We had to make a 100 a day, 4/6d per 100. I think my wages were 24 shillings per week, which was good money in them days. As an apprentice my work varied from working in the erecting and boiler shop, tool room, drawing office and machine shop on lathes.

At Highbridge Wharf I was part of a team that worked on the old steamships, *S S Julia* and *S S Radstock*. On the *Julia* we put in a new boiler, and on the *Radstock* we repaired the steam generator. Highbridge Wharf was a very busy port at that time, a considerable number of Scandinavian timber boats with wood stacked as high as the bridge came into Bland's yard.

Two types of S&D engines that I worked on were the 80 class and Johnsons. I would help strip them down rebuild them, and bore the cylinders on the 80 class. When I look back on it, there was a good variation of work at Highbridge, which helped me in future years. The engines and rolling stock which came out of the shops were a beautiful sight, dark blue paintwork created by craftsmen, five undercoats, three top coats, and then four coats of varnish were put on, and the S&D crest proudly showing through. It felt good to be part of this railway.

I recall an incident when I lost half a day's pay. There had been a robbery at Highbridge: somebody had stolen the safe from the Co-op. It had been dumped in the river just above our works. Divers were trying to recover it, so me and my mate decided to go and have a look at the action. We made our way to the scene to see all the fun, we were enjoying our grandstand view when a shout from behind caught our attention. We turned around quickly and there was the gaffer Harry Moorman. He wasn't pleased and sent us home and docked our pay.

One incident that I recall was when working with Teddy Fletcher in the erecting shop. There had been an accident at the far end of the shop, and Ted being a keen ambulance man went over to render assistance. When he got there he found the victim was his son; he died in Ted's arms. What had happened was that they were putting a new firebox into an 80 class and the lad had gone around to fetch something from the stores. When passing the engine, the smokebox door fell off onto him. It was found out later that the continuous hammering had undone the lugs on the smokebox door.

I had other members of my family on the S&D: my father was a passenger guard (he started at the goods shed at Wells and then moved to Highbridge – he felt there was a better opportunity at the works for us to learn a trade); I had two uncles, and my grandfather was also on the S&D. In fact my grandfather was one of the first pioneers of the S&D: he helped put the tracks down from Wells all the way down to the moors. He used to tell me how it was carried out; it was laid on trestles and built up from underneath.

I was enjoying my job at the works when the terrible news came through that Highbridge Works was to be closed down. Four hundred people worked there; this was 1930. It was a very sad year; my father died in April, and I went away to Nottingham in September to further my career. At the time if my mother had said "don't go" I wouldn't have done, but fortunately it worked out alright.

I spent 47 years on the railway working all over the north of England, as a senior engineer. I came back to my native home of Highbridge in 1970, to enjoy my retirement. My first days at Highbridge Works were the best.

Highbridge erecting shop in the 1920s: workshop staff pose in front of a 7F smokebox.
L–R: F Bennett, Sam Lane, C Williams, A Haines and P Lewis (Collection S Lane)

Bill May

I reported for work as a call and bar boy at Highbridge at 7am on Monday the 12th January 1920. I was met by the shed foreman Jim Braund, a very good man, and beside him was a chap my age who was going to show me what to do. They gave me an oil flare gun, a piece of sacking, wire brush, chipping hammer and an iron scraper. We climbed aboard this engine and opened the firehole doors and laid the sacking in the hole. He told me to get in feet first and he would follow. Our duty was to see the fire bars were in order then throw out any clinker that was left in the back of the firebox. We used the wire brush to clean off the tube ends and the crown stays of clinker, (this was called bar boys' work).

I had my mate for two days then he left me to go his own way. Once you had finished the firebox cleaning you went with others to cleaning the engines. After three weeks I was put on night duty which entailed engine cleaning and calling up the drivers and firemen for the early turn, which meant knocking on their doors where they lived. This had to be done one hour before signing on duty. This sometimes upset the neighbours as you knocked rather loudly to wake them up.

After three months I became a passenger cleaner. Drivers in them days had their own engines, and I cleaned for driver Bill Fry on passenger engine class 1P No 12. I took this over from Len Grant who moved on to be a passed cleaner. The engine had just had a general repair, and was freshly painted in the S&D blue. Your duties for these turns were three weeks of nights, and one week of days.

Things went smoothly along until the spring of 1924, when I was called into the office to see Mr Archbutt the superintendent, and asked if I was promoted to a passed cleaner would I move to Bath. I accepted the position and moved to Bath in March, where I stayed until the end of the summer workings and then returned to Highbridge. From then on things remained the same. I was doing as many firing turns as required when in 1930 Highbridge Works closed down which was a sad time for everybody in Highbridge. It affected so many lives.

The first two railwaymen to leave were R Larcombe, boilermaker, who moved to Kentish Town depot and B Dyer, foreman, who departed to Templecombe to take up a position as shedmaster. The end of April that year the engineering men from Highbridge Works went away to Derby. They left Highbridge on the 9.45am and we gave them a grand farewell. We had some unused detonators which we laid down on the track. It was a very sad occasion as the train disappeared out of sight; many a home was broken up that day.

The last person to leave Highbridge was Bill Luxton, a clerk, who cleared up the general office. When he finally closed the door in November 1930 he left a memorial card on the office door.

Just after the works closed, the carriage and wagon shop was turned into a piggery, and I remember Mr Alfred Whitaker, the locomotive superintendent who had the carriage and wagon shops built, having a look around the shops. His last words to Harry Moorman, our running foreman, was "I do not want to see it again, it has broken my heart to think it has come to this".

Just before the war the works was taken over by the government and used to store barbed wire and sandbags. The fields beside the main line had four receptions sidings and spurs for dumping material.

Burnham 27/10/51: driver Bill May and fireman Ray Gibbs bid farewell to an enthusiastic crowd on the occasion of the last passenger train to Highbridge (collection B May)

When the Americans came into the war it was handed over to them, and they brought their own steam engine.

My career moved on. I became a fireman in 1938, and a driver in 1943. I remember working a passenger train from Highbridge to Burnham-on-Sea. About half way we passed some clay pits which was a home for some swans. As we reached them these swans decided to wander onto the track. They made no effort to move so we had to stop the train and remove them.

BURNHAM-ON-SEA

Joan Fisher

My father Hugh Berryman was a porter at Burnham-on-Sea in 1924. As a young child I used to watch him pull the signal levers in the small cabin for the engines. At Burnham it was the end of the line so the engines would be uncoupled from the front of the train, run up to the seafront, back out to the home signal and then reverse onto the front of the train ready for the next trip to Highbridge. Sometimes if I was lucky I would have a ride on the footplate when this procedure was carried out (unofficial of course).

On Sundays there was a lot of holiday excursion traffic. I used to watch the hustle and bustle of holiday makers on the station while I was enjoying my Forte's ice cream.

Burnham: a special train stands in the closed station circa late 1950s. The loco is Ivatt tank No 41202 (Colin Caddy)

My father also had an allotment by the side of the railway; it was his way of relaxing and keeping us in fresh vegetables. Working on the railway in those days was totally different from today: on one occasion he didn't wear a tie on duty and had to attend a disciplinary hearing at Bath.

In Burnham father was well known for his home-made rhubarb wine. One Good Friday he had promised the local baker Bob Marchant a bottle of this lethal brew. Bob picked this bottle up in his motorbike and sidecar and made his way home, but he didn't arrive. A search party was sent out and they found him, his motorbike and sidecar in the ditch, minus the contents of the home made wine.

The family loved it at Burnham-on-Sea but if you wanted promotion you had to move, so in 1935 we said goodbye to Burnham and the family went to the coal fields of Radstock where father became a shunter working on the Sentinel engines.

COSSINGTON, BAWDRIP HALT & BRIDGWATER

Will Locke

Cossington station had a fine building with a stationmaster's house. Joining the station there were two sidings off the branch where coal, hay and other merchandise went for the villages of the Polden Hills. During the war Cossington station earnt a considerable amount of revenue from a nearby centre where blood was stored.

Cossington: a station view of 1912. A very substantial structure for such a small place (collection Will Locke)

Bawdrip Halt 1/3/52: the 9.40 Bridgwater– Edington Junction arrives with a Bulldog 3F 0-6-0 and a brake third (collection Will Locke)

Cossington station was beautifully situated on the brow of the Polden Hills; one could look down on the moorlands towards the sea as trains left Edington Junction towards Highbridge; you could see the smoke of the engine creeping towards Bason Bridge. As a boy I remember having picnics there and enjoying this lovely view with steam trains in the distance.

The porter at Cossington, George Peperall, lived in the station house. He had a large garden opposite the platform. He used to sell his produce to the local villagers and was also renowned for the repairing of boots and shoes.

Bawdrip halt had a small platform with a shelter on it. The station was situated on the side slopes of the Polden hills. One could get a lovely view from this spot of the rolling Somerset countryside. The halt was petitioned by the local vicar to the railway company and through his endeavours the halt was opened in 1923. It could accommodate three coaches. The line then went on through a cutting to Cossington station.

I have known many times when ladies with prams rushed onto the platform only to see the small tank engine moving out of the station. If the crew noticed this they would stop the train and reverse back into the halt to pick them up.

I started my railway service at Bridgwater on the S&D in April 1946. The Bridgwater branch was originally the Bridgwater Railway but it eventually came under the powers of the Somerset and Dorset. Men were proud to work on the railway at that time. Bridgwater was very busy when I joined. There was an enormous amount of goods traffic, various loads such as timber which took four men to manhandle with the help of a crane. The S&D had more than its share of revenue after the war, many Bridgwater firms producing goods for despatch. One such firm was the local brickwork company of Colthurst and Symons who sent large quantities of bricks around the country. This company also organized annual staff excursion trips from Bridgwater station to Blackpool and Southsea.

I recall a humorous occasion when a guard got off his train at Bridgwater and slipped over to the pub for a pint of ale. While he was enjoying his pint he had forgotten all about the time. It was dark and the engine crew looking out of the cab saw somebody waving and took it to be the guard and moved off to Edington Junction. The guard, realizing he was late, rushed back to the station to find no train. When the engine arrived at Edington it was quickly pointed out that the guard was not in his van. Frantic messages back and forth to Bridgwater meant that the footplate crew had to go back light engine to Bridgwater to pick up the guard. It was later found out that the signal the crew had seen was a friendly wave from the porter.

There were a few tunnels built on the branch to allow double lines but it came about that in latter years they were not needed. One of the sidings at Bridgwater was by the River Parrett; in its busier days there would be up to 45 wagons shunted in there.

There was a small signalbox at Bridgwater manned by Reg Carter and George Peperall. The stationmaster that I first met was Bert Oliver a very happy jovial man who would always greet you with a smile. The goods and station staff of Bridgwater were eight porters and one foreman and we all worked together as a team. The station was unusual as it was different from the normal railway stations, a bay platform with arrival and departure platforms. The station was a fair size with a parcel office room, ticket office, stationmaster's room and a porter's room. There used to be a big fair at Bridgwater: it was one of the largest in the country and there were lots of excursion trains coming in for this event. I remember one came in from Bath with eight coaches on which had to be shunted twice to get into the Bay. There was about three or four hundred people on these trains. I remember one gentleman returning from the fair who was carrying a large roll of lino and was trying to put it in a carriage full of people, it was quite amusing to watch.

Unfortunately passenger traffic came to an end at Bridgwater on Saturday 29th November 1952. I walked two miles in heavy snow to be one of the passengers on this last train. There was another three or four passengers, all

84

S&D railwaymen, on the train. We went out to Edington and on the return journey stopped at Cossington; nobody got on or off, it was a lonely station that night with only a couple of oil lamps twinkling through the darkness. We left the station and then stopped at Bawdrip halt. The guard got off the train and turned the oil lamp off; there was nobody there on the station, just an empty shelter on a deserted platform. The train moved on and we eventually came into Bridgwater station where we were met by a man who came especially to see the train. He mentioned to us that he saw the first train leave Bridgwater in 1890 and wanted to see the last S&D passenger train to come into Bridgwater. It was a very sad occasion. As I got off the train and made my way home in the snow and darkness, my thoughts were on the station and the way of life for me and many more people had now come to a end.

Fred Lester

After coming out of the RAF in 1947 I returned to the S&D Railway at Bridgwater. There was considerable commercial activity at that time despite the run down of the docks and wharf which had been such a source of freight in its heyday. Big timber importers' sheds lay alongside the station yard and long lines of wagons loaded with timber angled so that the overhanging ends came above the buffers. The wagons were regularly shunted across the road holding up the traffic. Wicker furniture, electric motors, bricks and jam were among the many diverse goods forwarded daily, and of course there was incoming goods for the shops and factories.

Life in the tiny goods office was always hectic, preparation of delivery documents for the morning deliveries was followed by hours of invoicing that had to be ready for the 6.30pm train in the evening. I travelled daily from Glastonbury on the 8.00am mixed train which consisted of one coach, five or six goods wagons and a brake van via Edington Junction, and returned on the 6.30pm (providing the branch train was not held up to wait for the main line at Highbridge – which often happened). Normally I would arrive home about 7.30pm.

Johnson 0-4-4 tank No 58072 awaiting departure from Bridgwater North with the 1.40pm to Edington Junction 5/9/52 (H C Casserley)

Percy Hobbs

During the war and a few years after we did a lodging turn to Bridgwater going down early morning and coming back the next day. This turn meant you signed on at 3.25am in the morning and got relieved by Bridgwater men at 11.45am. After a couple of pints at The Bird and Hand and a few hours rest we were back on at 8.45pm for the return trip. This was probably the shortest double turn in the country: 28 miles down and 28 miles back; we did two weeks of this straight off. It was a shunt, shunt, shunt duty all the way there and more on the home run. We were glad when they did away with this lodging turn.

In the summer time when it was very warm on the footplate there were plenty of points from Evercreech Junction to Highbridge where you could pop just outside to a nearby pub and get a nice cool pint of bitter. The men treated this with respect and kept well within the limits.

POLSHAM HALT

Polsham 1912 with all the usual items on the platform – barrow, milk churns… but no seats! (Lens of Sutton)

Fred Lester

Polsham Halt was on the branch line between Wells and Glastonbury. It was a combined halt and level crossing with gates and locking signals controlled by a small ground frame. There was a crossing keeper's cottage, always referred to as the station house because of the small platform. It was occupied for many years by Stan Ford and his wife. He was a well known local character in the area. He began his career on the S&D as a lad porter at Wells Priory Road in my dad's time, and later drove a goods delivery vehicle. The gates have long gone but there is still a nice little house for its present owners which I'm happy to say is called the "Station House" today.

WELLS

Paul Fry

I lived in the station house during the war years at Wells Priory Road and I remember a runaway train. The incident related to a Government store train that was in transit from Witham on the GWR line coming through Shepton Mallet to Wells, eventually destined for Highbridge where there was a big

United States depot. The train consisted of about thirty open wagons sheeted, which contained five-gallon jerry cans of high octane fuel, which was being stored at Highbridge. The train left Shepton Mallet with the inspector on board and it was decided that it would travel down the bank into Wells without pinning down the brakes, as the inspector was rather concerned that if any of them got hot they may have had problems with a fire. The driver and the guard decided they could hold them on the bank and away they went. Unfortunately away they went indeed: they ran away down the bank heading towards Wells. The situation at Wells was that on the approach to Wells you came across the level crossing at Priory Road, through Priory Road station, then the line forked, one line going to Glastonbury and onto Highbridge and the other one went through Wells Tucker Street station (which was the old Great Western station), going onto Wookey and Yatton. Now the thing was that the train ran away down the bank and the signalman at the GWR East Somerset box, just on the upside of the level crossing, heard the train whistling that it was running away and in trouble so he sent the "train running away" to the next signalbox which was a Somerset and Dorset box.

He opened the gates and stood back and let the train go through. The signalman at the S&D box at Priory Road (I must point out that even in this late time the GWR and S&D signalmen didn't normally mix; they both enjoyed a pint in The Railway Hotel; the GWR men had their pint of ale in the front saloon bar and the S&D men had theirs in the side bar)... anyway the S&D signalman had a decision to make regarding this runaway petrol train, whether to send this train to Glastonbury which was on a dropping gradient or to send it through to the Tucker Street GWR station on towards Wookey. He chose the latter and the train shot through Priory Road station at a high rate of speed, and ended up almost at Wookey before the rising gradient pulled it to a stop with brake blocks burnt out and everybody thoroughly shaken up.

Of course there was an enquiry after this. An inspecting officer held this in the waiting room at Priory Road station. He interviewed the GWR signalman of the East Somerset box and congratulated him on his prompt action in opening the gates and allowing the runaway train through. He said it would be put onto his record as good conduct. It came then to the S&D signalman of Priory Road who was summoned before the inspecting officer. The inspector asked him why he had chosen to send the train to Tucker Street GWR station rather than send it through to the S&D station of Glastonbury, the inspector asked him did he feel that there was a train coming from Glastonbury and this may have caused problems?

The Somerset and Dorset signalman thought for some little while and then with a very succinct answer said "Well, 'twas the Western's train so I let 'em have 'em"!

I used to live in the station house, Priory Road, and spent most of my time speaking to the porters and booking clerks. I remember one evening in 1942 being in the booking office when suddenly the door opened and an apparition appeared in the doorway. Wells being a cathedral city had many a visiting clergyman who would alight at Priory Road station. This particular evening was very dark and the clergyman had got off the train coming down from Shepton Mallet. Obviously because of the war there was no lights visible, so he made his way down the platform and unfortunately he fell down into the cattle dock. When he appeared in the doorway of the booking office he was covered from head to foot in cow manure and was very irate. His first words upon entering the booking office were "I've just fallen down a bloody great hole". At that the booking office clerk and porter dissolved into tears of laughter. The clergyman was not impressed and later he put in a claim for his clerical suit to be cleaned.

Eric Miles

My first permanent post as a signalman was at Wells Priory Road in November 1949. I was at Blandford on temporary relief when the call came to go to Wells. I was given the day off to visit the signalbox; the signalman who was leaving was a grand old gent in his 70s, who was asked to stay on as no one in those days wanted the job. I had to find accommodation. It was very tricky to find a place near the station, but I eventually obtained lodgings with the widow of a former stationmaster who knew all the needs and difficult hours of the railway. After about a fortnight I was considered competent to take over the duties; there were two split shifts; not long after taking over duties in the box my opposite number left to take over another box leaving me to work both shifts. Not that it worried me as it meant overtime and no platform work; the Western region took over the goods shed and yard so we had S&D and Western shunting, there was plenty of interesting work.

The first duty was to switch in the box (5-5-5 beats on the block bell) put a switch to half-way position, replace signals to on position then put switch to full open position. This was of course to the other two Western boxes, the 5-5-5 bell signal (opening of signalbox) being sent to Glastonbury box on the token instrument bell. The move was for the S&D loco to travel the goods yard (Western) over the level crossing worked from East Somerset box to collect wagons, left there by the early Western goods from Bristol. These were then marshalled on the rear of the first passenger train to Glastonbury.

One of the duties of the signalman was to inform the porter in charge of Polsham Halt (the only station between Wells and Glastonbury) that the train was either leaving Wells or Glastonbury. At the end of the day the engine was taken to the shed after placing the passenger coach into the sidings, the signalbox was then switched out to Glastonbury (7-5-5 beats on token instrument bell), the closing procedure given to the two Western boxes (Tucker Street and Wells East Somerset), the closing switch being operated and applicable stop signals lowered to enable the Western trains to run.

There was no Sunday working but we did have two specials to Bournemouth, two coaches being started from Glastonbury. One thing that stands out during my stay at Wells signalbox was the christening of "The City of Wells" loco, this being performed by the Bishop of Bath and Wells. All the staff at the time at Wells were given 2s 6d.

My saddest moment was when the line closed between Wells and Glastonbury in 1951. The last train of the day arrived to the explosion of detonators. It disappeared into the distance to Glastonbury, leaving me to give 2-2-1 beats on the bell for the last time on the branch.

Next page: a silent scene – Wells 16/4/65. The S&D station 13 years after closure (Colin Caddy)